CZECH
MATE

CZECH MATE

David Hathaway

Fleming H. Revell Company
Old Tappan, New Jersey

This book was originally published in Great Britain by
LAKELAND, 116 Baker Street, London

Scripture quotations in this book are from the King James
Version of the Bible.

"The Rabbits Who Caused All the Trouble" and "The Very
Proper Gander " are by James Thurber, and are used by permission
of Helen Thurber. Copyright © 1940 James Thurber.
Copyright © 1968 Helen Thurber. From FABLES FOR OUR TIME,
published by Harper & Row. Originally printed in THE NEW YORKER.

The chorus from the hymn, "How Great Thou Art," by Carl
Boberg, Stuart K. Hine, Translator, is Copyright © 1955 by Manna
Music, Inc., 2111 Kenmere Ave., Burbank, CA 91504 International
Copyright Secured. All Rights Reserved. Used by Permission.

Library of Congress Cataloging in Publication Data

Hathaway, David.
    Czech mate.

    1. Hathaway, David.   2. Bible — Publication and distribution
— Europe, Eastern.   3. Prisoners — Czechoslovak Republic.
I Title.
BR1725.H245A33 1975   266'.3'0924 [B]   75-6552
ISBN 0-8007-0742-7

CONTENTS

1

ARREST AT THE IRON CURTAIN

It was just four o'clock in the morning by my watch when they ordered me out of the chair where I was trying to snatch a little rest and took me into an adjoining room. Almost immediately a man whom I already knew to be a senior officer of the state security police came in, put his hand on my shoulder, and told me I was under arrest. Unlike the others, he was not in uniform, just dressed in a plain brown suit. He did not speak English, so everything was done through an interpreter whose translation, if not perfect, was at least intelligible. Up till now the interrogation had been firm and correct though, deprived of food, drink, and sleep, my mind was in a haze.

I looked at Brown Suit; his sparse, graying hair was brushed severely back, his lined and wrinkled face betrayed no feeling or emotion. So far, his total knowledge of English had seemed to be "Bobby Charlton," but in this moment of extreme tension he summoned up his last reserve of the language and enunciated slowly, *"Football . . . two . . . nil."* I was trembling a little, partly from weariness and lack of food, and also with the chill of the night air. I was still unable to take in everything that had happened, and even the armed guard set to watch me with a pistol in his belt seemed unreal.

It seemed a long time since yesterday morning when I

had awakened in the Hotel Strauss in the familiar West German town of Wurzburg. We had only recently discovered the pleasant hotel with its comfortable beds and good food, though for two years we had been routing our long-distance bus tours through this interesting medieval town. I had breakfasted with the passengers, loaded the baggage, and with a prayer for God's blessing we had set off on day three of the tour which would terminate in a beautiful Black Sea coastal resort in Rumania. We were looking forward to the golden sands, the warm sunshine and, at this time of year especially, the sea which was beautiful for bathing. That Wednesday, June 21, 1972 (Midsummer Day as I was later to recollect), was warm and sunny as we left our hotel for the leisurely run to Prague. This was to be my first visit to Czechoslovakia. I was familiar with all the other countries on our route, Austria, Hungary, Yugoslavia, Rumania, but this was new territory to me, and the prospect intrigued me. The last time Crusader Tours had taken a group there had been in 1968, just before the uprising, and we were only now including it again in our itinerary.

We were to cross the border at Rozvadov. The West German formalities were stricter than usual, which surprised but did not alarm me. The Czech frontier itself was like many others I had seen, with its barbed wire, guard towers, and soldiers armed with rifles and machine guns. David Lowth, our driver, took the bus slowly down the road, squeezed across a narrow bridge which was just wide enough for the large vehicle, then stopped; the traffic-control barrier was down, and armed guards indicated that we would have to wait.

Something seemed to be going on in front. I stepped down from the bus and moved over to the left to get a better view. The bus in front of us was being thoroughly searched. The guards had ordered the passengers out and were stripping it down, removing baggage and everything movable. Then, still not satisfied, they began a minute examination of the bodywork.

I experienced an unusual rush of panic. I wanted desperately to tell our driver to turn around and go back, but that was impossible; the bus was thirty-six feet long and we were on a narrow road with an even narrower bridge behind us. By now, inevitably, the traffic had piled up at our rear, so that we could not possibly reverse. Why did I feel so uneasy? This tour was no different from many I had led before. Our passports were in order, the visas, obtained in London before our departure, were unquestionably valid, the hotel accommodation in Prague had been paid for in advance. All arrangements had been made through the London office of Čedok, the state-owned travel agency which had arranged everything, including the two guides who were waiting for us.

When at last the barrier lifted and we were waved forward, I still felt a little sick and apprehensive. . . .

And so they had searched the bus, had found what they were looking for, and they had arrested me. It was now just after six o'clock, and the interrogation was beginning all over again.

"Tell us exactly what happened after you left England."

"Where did you stay on Tuesday night?"

"Why are you coming to visit Czechoslovakia?"

"Who put the Bibles in the bus?"

Ah . . . the Bibles. They wanted to know who had loaded nearly three thousand Bibles in the bus, and what we intended to do with them. Didn't we know it was forbidden to bring these books into the country? (In fact, there is no law forbidding the import of Bibles into Czechoslovakia. The Communists claim religious freedom, therefore, they will not put on the law books any law which exposes this claim as fraud. For this reason, I never felt I was breaking their law. You cannot break a law which doesn't exist.)

Who had put them on the bus? I had already told them, truthfully enough, that I hadn't. I was becoming confused from lack of sleep, hunger, constant questioning for hour after hour . . . what wouldn't I give for a cup of tea . . . let me lie down for just a few minutes . . . I don't know, I can't tell you . . . surely they can't keep us, we are tourists. . . . Slowly I tried to pull myself together. Two things were clear, I was under arrest, and they didn't believe I was telling the truth.

I had stuck strictly to my story, which was true, that there were no Bibles on the bus when we left England, that we had arrived at the Hotel Strauss at approximately six o'clock on Tuesday evening. I had had dinner about seven, spent the remainder of the evening doing some routine maintenance work on the bus with the driver, then gone into the hotel for a chat over a soda with some of the passengers. Some German tourists sitting at a neighboring table had questioned me in fluent English about our itinerary (there were two other bus parties besides ours in the hotel that night). There was no secrecy about this, since it was published in one of our supplementary programs. At about eleven o'clock, David Lowth went to bed. I was waiting for some friends, but when they had not turned up by midnight, I want to bed, too, rather tired because the previous night had been spent on the cross-channel ferry from Dover to Zeebrugge, with not much sleep.

All this I had told my interrogators; the only thing I dared not tell them was the fact that when I went to bed I left the key of the bus with two of the passengers, Will Dickerson and Peter Harvey, with full instructions as to what to do when my friends arrived. These two had travelled with me on a number of previous occasions, and knew the procedure exactly. Obviously I could not reveal this to the secret police, who nevertheless made it quite clear to me that, although I had denied loading any Bibles, since I was the owner of the bus and of the travel company, it was my responsibility and I was the one who would be punished.

What would they do to me? I was a British subject and had not yet technically entered their country. Surely the most they would do would be to confiscate the Bibles and possibly the bus; I was convinced they would soon release me and the passengers.

The day wore on, the sun warming the chill out of the atmosphere, but doing nothing to alleviate the bleakness of the upstairs corridor where I spent most of the next few hours. I saw the passengers taken in one by one for interrogation. There was an interlude during which some men brought in movie cameras and, fixing up special lighting, proceeded to film me surrounded by Bibles and other baggage. With the later addition of pictures of the bus, they were able to make a thirty-five-minute television documentary with a commentary showing me as an agent of the West bringing subversive literature into their country. Yet the Czech authorities claim to freely print Bibles. If my Bibles were "subversive" what about theirs?

Several times I managed to look out the window to see if there was any possibility of escape, but always the watchful presence of my guard prevented any such move. I wished, futilely, that I had taken one of several opportunities that had offered themselves the previous day, before they put this armed guard on me.

When they had first discovered the Bibles, they had taken David Lowth away for questioning but left me with the passengers quite free to walk about. As late as ten o'clock in the evening I had still thought that we would soon be released, in fact I had spent those hours trying to persuade one of the officials to telephone our hotel and get hold of the guide who was waiting for us. They never did so. Then I tried to negotiate for us to be allowed to continue on to Prague and for the interrogation to be continued there if necessary. It was all useless; they understood little English and at that stage did not bother to bring in an interpreter. I became so concerned and desperate that at one point I considered turning the bus and attempting to cross back over the border, or at least escaping myself. But there were the passengers to consider, and in any case, if I succeeded in taking the bus and passengers, I did not want to leave the driver. Now, it looked as though all hope of escaping was over for me.

Late in the afternoon they allowed me to speak to the bus driver, to make some decision as to what should happen to the rest of the tour. It seemed as if the others were going to be allowed to leave, without me. Not surprisingly, they preferred not to continue to Prague, despite the invitation of the Czech police to sample more of the country's hospitality, but decided to return to West Germany and go on from there to Vienna.

I watched from the upstairs window as, twenty-eight hours after we had arrived at the border, the bus with the passengers drove slowly away. I knew how sick David Lowth was feeling, hating to abandon me to the mercy of the police, yet anxious to take himself and the passengers as far from them as possible, and back into safety. As I saw them disappear around the bend in the road, my heart sank; now my last link with the West was broken. Suddenly I felt physically sick, trembling for a moment, fearful of what the Communists might now do to me. Would I ever see my wife Zena and the children again? There was little Mandy, only three years old and now without a father. What would happen to my travel company? This was the busiest time of the year, and I was due back to lead other tours. Surely it would cause a stir back in England when I failed to return — but would I ever get out of this country alive?

About an hour later, around eight o'clock, one of the guards came in and motioned to me to go downstairs. I was bundled into the back seat of a car with my baggage — they had taken everything off the bus that could be in any way connected with me, things which were mine and things which were not mine. The interpreter squeezed in beside me and one of the interrogators sat in front with the driver. I noticed he was armed.

We set off at high speed, travelling so fast that three times I felt sure the car would overturn on a corner. Desperately I looked out of the windows, trying to catch sight of some landmark, signpost, or any indication of where we were going, but without success. Eventually, after about an hour, we ran through the outskirts of a town. I saw the high walls of a prison; then massive gates, surrounded by machine-gun towers, swung open to receive the car which came to a halt in the courtyard. I was led across rough cobbles, up stone steps, and through big wooden doors into the main prison building. Here the escort and the interpreter left me, the big doors swung shut, and I was alone in that gloomy building with 2,500 other prisoners and the guards, not one of whom spoke English.

They made me undress, took away all my personal possessions including my watch, and gave me a rough prison uniform. They indicated that I should sign the forms that they made out, listing all the various items which they had confiscated; but since I could not understand what was written, I simply had to sign and hope for the best. Then they marched me down a long corridor towards the interior of the building. We passed through several iron gates, every one of which the officer opened

13

with a key and then locked behind us. As each door crashed shut, any hope of ever getting out of this place became more remote. It was night by now, and by the gloomy light of electric bulbs I could see other corridors radiating out from a central hub before my guard selected one and led me to yet another locked door which barred our way.

It was only then that the full horror of what had happened dawned on my numbed mind. I suddenly realized that at that precise moment nobody in the West knew where I was. I had not yet learned that this was Bory prison in Pilsen, the most infamous jail in Czechoslovakia. All I knew was that I was inside one of the dreaded Communist prisons. How many braver men than I had died here? What methods of interrogation would they use on me before they finished with me? I felt hot tears stinging my eyes — "Oh, God, what will happen to me?"

We climbed some stairs to the first floor, where my guard opened the door of cell number thirty-one, motioning me roughly to enter. As soon as I had stumbled through the door it was slammed and locked behind me. There was barely room for me to get in. In a space thirteen feet by six, four iron beds were placed side by side, on which four men lay on mattresses of inch-thick plastic foam. As there was no bed for me, they made room for me in the middle and I lay down among them to get what rest I could. They knew no English, I couldn't speak one word of Czech. I tried a few words in French, then German, but I was so exhausted that my befuddled brain could not cope with their replies. I was confused and shocked, and though I tried to sleep, the realization of my position was like a waking nightmare, aggravated by the electric light which was left on all night.

Dawn came, and after two more dragging hours a loud, penetrating buzzer sounded — a noise with which I was to become all too familiar in the coming days and weeks. My cellmates dragged themselves out of their uncomfortable and cramped positions and began to put on their ragged prison uniforms. I did the same — what else could I do? After a further wait a key grated in the lock and the door was flung open. Breakfast was served. The other prisoners rushed to take cans of nauseating coffee substitute — known to the prisoners as Nafta, the Czech name for fuel oil — and a hunk of dark brown bread. In spite of my hunger, I couldn't face the bread. I must confess that in six months I only attempted it about ten times, and I certainly didn't that first morning.

I had hardly time to swallow my coffee before they came for me. As I followed my guard along the iron gangway, down the stone steps to the corridor, I was able for the first time to see something of the prison layout. The cells were on three floors with iron balconies, with a safety net between them. The ground floor was paved with large stone slabs and the gloomy, foul-smelling corridor was dimly lit by a window at one end and an occasional light bulb which showed up the dirty stonework, peeling paint, and crumbling plaster.

Across the central hub, past other prisoners who either ignored or glanced suspiciously at me as we passed. Along corridors, with every few yards the ritual of unlocking and locking doors. In the main block; through the gates; up the stairs to the third floor; into the third room on the left. The room itself was pleasant enough, with a large window overlooking the prison walls to freedom beyond, painted walls, plain but tidy. It was furnished with two desks and three chairs; piled on one side were Bibles and other confiscated literature along with some of my personal effects and luggage.

The interrogation seemed endless. There were continuous questions asked through the interpreter, then at the end, when all the questioning was finished, the chief interrogator typed out his summary of the information he was demanding. This was then translated back to me and I was asked to sign it. I refused, because it did not conform to the statements that I had made and was based only on what they wanted to state themselves.

At last the guards were summoned again and I was taken back to my cell. Obviously they were not pleased with me because I was not cooperating. A short while later, the guards were back, this time curtly indicating that I must gather up my things and leave the cell. I had a few moments of wild hope. Were they going to let me go, after all? But all they did was take me across the corridor into cell fifty-four. Here I found myself with a West German, Alex, and two Czech boys. Realizing my plight they really did everything they could to help me. My limited knowledge of German was a tremendous help, for again, they did not speak one word of English.

The next day, Saturday, the procedure was the same: out for interrogation, then back to the cell when it was over. I was thankful to discover that they did not work on Sunday; although they had no respect for the Sabbath, they obviously liked their weekends free. For me, accustomed to regular family worship, that day was particularly hard. I kept thinking of my family back at home, then of the service I had attended the previous Sunday, little knowing that within a week I would have become simply a number in a Communist prison. How slowly those hours passed! Conversation was a real problem; at that time it was merely a matter of basic communication. We were not allowed to climb up and look out of the window; if we were caught we could lose some of our few privileges, like letters from home, or parcels. But I did not know this yet, and especially on that first long Sunday I climbed up so many times to press my face against the bars. . . . .

Outside was the fresh air of freedom. We appeared to be on the outskirts of a large town and over the prison wall I could see green trees, the movement of an occasional car. Then my ear caught the sound of birdsong and my straining eyes located him as he soared high up into the blue of the sky. That bird seemed to me to be the symbol of freedom. As I looked and listened, I thought in despair of the events of the last few days and hours. My mind rebelled against all that had happened. I was frantic to get out; crushed by the smallness of the cell, oppressed by the bars at the window, the sight of the locked door, even the sounds of the prison; the last straw was the strange babel of sound that surrounded me, for my companions were speaking a language I had never heard before, and it made my confusion and loneliness complete. As I looked back over recent events there seemed to be so many ifs and buts. Why had it happened to me? What if I had managed to turn around at the border? Why had I chosen to route this particular trip through Czechoslovakia? . . . why? . . . why? . . . why? . . . Until there came the now familiar sound of a turning key and with a clattering of aluminum cans the watery soup that was part of our lunch was pushed in through the doorway of the cell.

Monday morning. Later, I was to remember this as "Black Monday," largely because for the first time the veneer of communism was stripped off to show the true face beneath.

Shortly after breakfast, the guards came for me. More interrogation. They began firing questions at me.

"You are a believer?" This was more of a statement than a question.

"Of course I am." I had no wish to deny it.

"Then are you a Catholic?"

"No."

"Are you a *Protestanti*?"

17

Thinking that the question was simple enough, I replied in the affirmative. I was not to discover until later that in the Czech language the word *protestanti* means, literally translated, a militant protester against the regime; in other words a political agitator. Eventually, when it came to my trial, the prosecutor was to allege that I had confessed my own guilt. This was typical of the way in which the interrogator could distort my replies to prove almost anything he desired.

The next question: "You brought three thousand Bibles into our country. Tell us the names and addresses of the believers who were to receive them."

"I do not know these names and addresses."

"You are lying. Tell us their names, or it will be the worse for you."

"I am telling you the truth. I don't know."

"You filthy Christian . . . you are lying to us."

By now they realized that they were not getting anywhere with the interrogation. There was a pause for a while, then the door opened and in walked Brown Suit, the SVD chief whom I had first met at the border. There was no smile to break the severity of his lined features, as he walked briskly into the room and began to speak rapidly and sharply in Czech.

"Tell us the names of the Czech believers who were to receive the Bibles."

"I am sorry, but I do not know the names of any Czech people."

"Then what were you going to do with the Bibles?" (It was four months before I learned that actually there were only 139 Czech Bibles; the others were in Russian, Hungarian, Rumanian, and other languages. I had not loaded them and so was not aware of the exact contents.)

What could I say? I prayed silently and briefly for help. Then I realized that by now it was five days since my arrest and it would be safe to tell the truth.

"Some other men from West Germany were to follow me over the border. I was to give the Bibles to them and they would distribute them. They knew the addresses, not me."

"Where were you to meet them?" barked the interpeter.

"Outside the office of Čedok, in Wenceslas Square in Prague."

"I warn you, do not try to make jokes."

"I am telling the truth."

I was becoming more confident, with the thought that my contacts would by now certainly have left the country. They would have guessed I had been arrested when I did not turn up for the rendezvous on Wednesday. Also, miraculously, a couple of hours after the original discovery of the Bibles I had been waiting by the bus, and had actually seen one of our other vehicles come through the border and had surreptitiously given the driver the thumbs-down sign.

It was fortunate that I had not revealed this information any sooner for, as I was later to discover, the police immediately checked to see if any tourists who had crossed on the same day as me were were still in the country. However, they made one vital mistake. They assumed that, because my support personnel came from West Germany, they were German, but in fact they were of various nationalities. They never located them.

It seemed my story was too much for Brown Suit to swallow.

"We know you are lying," he shouted at me through the interpreter. "But we will make you tell the truth. Tell us the names of the Czech people who were to receive the Bibles. You will only make it worse for yourself if you refuse."

"I can't tell you, I don't know," I insisted. In any case

19

I had no doubts as to what would happen to any Czech citizens if I gave their names.

By now Brown Suit was really mad at me. He began to storm up and down, hardly able to contain himself.

"You are lying. You are an enemy of our state. People try to bring many things across our borders. Some bring drugs, others pornographic literature, but you . . . you are guilty of bringing these filthy, offensive books which attack our state and pervert the minds of the people. This is a very serious crime, and you will be punished severely.

"There was a time," he continued, "when prisoners were tortured to make them talk. We no longer use those methods." He paused significantly. "We have more sophisticated means."

There was a long pause during which someone began firing an automatic rifle outside the window.

When the message had had time to sink in, he began again in a tone that was not lost on me, despite the interpreter: "You will go back to your cell, you can stay there until you rot, until you die for all we care. We will not open the door to talk to you. You will not be allowed to come out and talk to us. We are not interested in you anymore. You will rot in your cell and die there unless or until you call us, begging and pleading to be allowed to tell us everything we want to know."

I realized what that meant. I have spoken personally to prisoners who spent up to two years in these interrogation departments. They do not need to torture you at that stage. If you are a married man with a family and you have a business, how long can you hold out when you know it can go on for months or years without trial? I was really frightened.

He summoned the guards, who dragged me back across the prison to my cell. They opened the door, I was pushed in, and once more heard the terrifying sound of the turning key. Perhaps I would never see my wife and children again. Perhaps I would die in here, with no one to care. It was the most terrible moment of my life. The end of a chapter . . . perhaps the end of the whole. Over the weeks and months that followed I was to see the methods that they used, to see young men in their twenties turn gray under the strain, to know of some who tried to commit suicide. It seemed it was the end for me. . . .

2

THE COMMUNIST FRONTIER OPENS

I looked around my cell . . . at the iron-barred window . . . the rough painted walls . . . the bare floor. . . . So this is what it is like to be in a prison. But why was I here? Was it really eleven years ago that I had first crossed the Iron Curtain? Seen for the first time what lay beyond?

There had been nine of us in a yellow-painted Commer minibus which rolled up to the Yugoslav border in May 1961. We travelled via Belgrade and Nis before climbing the unpaved road which ran between remote villages and over the hills towards the Dragoman Pass and the Bulgarian border. We looked apprehensively ahead as our eyes took in the forbidding panorama of barbed wire, minefields, and armed guards with dogs, which seemed designed either to keep us out or worse, when we had crossed, to prevent any possibility of our escape back to freedom. All of us admitted afterwards that we were afraid. Westerners were treated with open suspicion in those days, and although we had taken the obvious precaution of obtaining visas in advance in London, it was clear to us that not many tourists ventured across the forbidding borders of what is still often called "Little Russia."

We were on our way from England to Israel to attend an international Christian conference in Jerusalem. I was then, as I am still, intensely interested in developments in the Middle East and the way in which modern events are fulfilling the old biblical prophecies, and I was determined to take this opportunity to visit the Holy Land. There was only one big problem — how could I raise the fare?

It was then that I looked at a map and realized it should be perfectly possible to drive all the way. Physically, there were few obstacles. Politically, though, there were two major barriers. The most serious seemed to be the fact that the Syrians did not allow travellers to cross from their country into Israel. This was overcome by the simple expedient of using two passports and duplicate customs documents. The other problem, of getting through Bulgaria, we decided to play by ear, once we had gotten our visas.

At the border, officials took away our passports and visas for scrutiny, then we had to stand and wait while the frontier guards made a thorough search of the bus, taking out most of our carefully packed food and camping gear, obviously looking for something, yet never telling us what. Finally, after what seemed one of the longest hours we had ever spent, they seemed satisfied and allowed us to continue our journey.

By this time we were tired, and were glad to be able to drive on the few miles to Sofia where we spent a short time before looking for the campsite where we were to stay the night. It lay on our direct route out of the city, on the road towards Turkey and Istanbul, and did not take us long to find. To our horror and surprise it looked more like a concentration camp than a holiday site, surrounded by high barbed-wire fences and entered through massive iron gates.

On arrival, we had to surrender our passports, and as darkness fell, after we had pitched our tents, the gates were locked and we realized with some trepidation that they were taking no chances with us. We were virtually prisoners. Any possibility of getting out was out of the question. We consoled ourselves with the thought that these precautions were only to prevent us from wandering off during the night to do a bit of bourgeois Western sightseeing, or what they would call "espionage."

Sheer physical weariness ensured for us a sound night's sleep, and we were immensely relieved the following morning to find the gates open and our passports ready to be collected. In spite of a strict warning not to deviate from the route we had filed with the authorities, we sur-reptitiously retraced our course into the center of Sofia, our minds full of curiosity and our cameras of Koda-chrome. Having satiated the former and exposed the latter we continued our journey without really relaxing the ten-sion until late that afternoon we reached the Turkish bor-der, where again we were subjected to a most rigorous search before being allowed to cross out of the country. It was with an indescribable sense of relief that we once again breathed the free (though odorous) air and were able to express ourselves freely (if we could make ourselves heard above the cacophony of sound which assailed us from every quarter).

This journey marked a major milestone in my life. It was the first time in modern years that anyone had made the overland crossing by road from Britain to Israel — we beat by three months a similar expedition by a party from Cambridge University. It also led directly into the founda-tion of my travel company, Crusader Tours, and was the first of many incidents which culminated in my imprison-ment in a Czechoslovak jail.

I began organizing other parties, small ones at first, of likeminded people who wanted to visit Israel. Our objec-tive at first was entirely to tour the Holy Land itself, but of course we always had to pass through Bulgaria. With the increasing frequency of my visits behind the Iron Curtain I was lulled into a sense of blindness as to what was happening there. I saw no signs of persecution of believers, no evidence of closed churches nor of secret or underground meetings. It was so easy for us to accept what we were shown and to believe that it represented a true picture of life in these countries, as it still does for visitors today.

So it came as a real shock to me when in 1963 Pastor Haralan Popov was released from prison in Bulgaria, and came to the West to tell of his experiences. I remembered hearing that he was the pastor of the largest Evangelical church in Bulgaria. In fact, my father had known him as long ago as 1938. Because of his activities in the church and his faithful witness for Christ, he was sentenced by the Communists to fifteen years in prison. Later, I was to learn of such underground pastors as Stefan Bankov, who was serving the believers of closed churches. Thus, rather belatedly, my eyes were opened to what was happening in these countries which I visited so innocently. I was shaken by the realization that, even while I was taking parties of tourists through, Christians were suffering or even dying for their faith. I began to pray that God would open up ways in which I could help these suffering believers.

Meanwhile a major crisis occurred in my personal life. I could not understand why I kept losing my voice. It was partcularly inconvenient, since at that time I was still pastor of a congregation in Dewsbury in England, where I had been since the end of 1959. My doctor tried various medicines, without any obvious success. At last he sent me to see a specialist at the local hospital. I went along at the appointed time with no real concern, even perhaps with a vague hope that he might recommend a long rest. So it came as a rather sudden shock when, after a careful examination, he told me there was a growth on a vocal cord, probably malignant, and that I must have an immediate operation.

Although he stressed that the matter was urgent, I asked for time to consider. He agreed to give me a month. I went away, still dazed with the suddenness of the whole thing, and it was only when I got home and talked it over with my wife that I realized the full seriousness of what I had been told.

Over the next month I spent hours in prayer, asking God to heal me by a miracle. I believed He could, and indeed I had known instances of miraculous healings. I knew that, if He wanted to, He could remove the growth so that an operation would prove unnecessary. Towards the end of the time I felt so confident I was healed that I asked for another appointment with the specialist to confirm the fact. My doctor, a skeptic, agreed, on condition that if the growth was still there, as he firmly believed it would be, I would offer no further objection to an immediate operation; for, as he rightly pointed out, delay could be serious and would only necessitate a larger section of the vocal cord being removed.

Confidently I went back to the hospital. To my dismay, the specialist only confirmed that the growth was increasing in size, and that immediate attention was necessary. Unable to accept the inevitable, I begged for yet more time, until somewhat reluctantly he agreed to a further month; but this was to be final, no further delay was possible.

Now I knew I was involved in a crucial battle. There was the increasing possibility that an operation might take away the whole of the vocal vord, leaving me with no voice whatsoever. This, for a preacher, was unthinkable. I began to pray more urgently.

But another factor kept intruding itself. The tours to the Holy Land, which had started in a small way, were begin-

26

ning to attract more business than I could cope with in addition to my duties as pastor of a church. The time was fast approaching when I would have to make a final decision. Either I must cut down on my pastoral work and concentrate on my growing interest in the lands of the Bible and the prophetical implications of modern events in Israel, or I must put an end to this division of loyalties and give my whole time to my church duties. I channelled prayer desperately in both directions, in an effort to resolve what had suddenly become a very immediate and pressing crisis.

My prayers for a miracle crystallized into a set pattern. I found myself constantly saying the same thing: "O God, I know You *can* heal, because of all the evidence of Your Word, as well as the other miracles which I have seen with my own eyes. But . . . the problem is . . . You can`. . . if You want to. . . . Is it really Your will to heal *me*?" At the same time I was asking Him to show me what He wanted me to do with regard to the future.

Eventually I made what seemed a rather dangerous and difficult decision. But strangely, I felt a real sense of peace in my mind when I had done it. I now prayed clearly and positively: "O God, show me Your definite will and plan for my life in this way. If You want me to stay in charge of the church, which would seem to most people the obvious thing, then do not heal me, let things take their natural course and let me face the operation and all that may follow without any intervention. But if You definitely want me to give up the security of my pastorate and take up as full-time occupation this interest in the Holy Land, with all its uncertainties, then I ask You to intervene and interrupt the natural course of this disease by completely and miraculously healing me."

Now there was only one question instead of *two.* My problems had combined and consolidated, so that my prayer became simply: "Tell me if it is Your will to intervene and heal me or not." It was a cold, wintry day in December when I reached this point, a Wednesday as I recall. There was still no answer, but the final appointment with the specialist was the next day. Five o'clock in the evening found me on my knees in my bedroom. If only I could know positively what the will of God was, I felt, I would be satisfied. In desperation I turned to a promise box, pulled out one of the little slips of paper and read Romans 8:28: "All things work together for good to them that love God." "No," I cried, "that isn't what I want. I know that already. All I am asking for is a positive yes or no." I picked up my Bible and looked up the verse in its context. I read from verses 26 and 27, "We know not what we should pray for as we ought: but the Spirit itself maketh intercession for us . . . according to the will of God." That was it! It came with certainty to me that God had said yes. I would be healed by a miracle.

The next morning I looked forward eagerly to my appointment with the specialist. He put various instruments down my throat, examined me for a long time and very carefully, before turning to me with a serious expression. "I can't understand what has happened," he said, "but the growth has gone. There is a scar there as though it had been cut out with a knife. Well, your faith has been vindicated."

I could hardly wait to get home to tell Zena, I was so excited, but first I called in to tell my own doctor, who had been so skeptical throughout about miracles and answers to prayer. His jaw dropped in astonishment, he was completely at a loss for words.

Now that God had intervened to reverse the natural progression of this growth and heal me, I knew beyond a doubt that it was also His will that I should concentrate on my tours to the Holy Land. Zena and I formed a travel company, which we called Crusader Tours, and I gave up the church pastorate to concentrate on this new and exciting work to which God had called me.

3

A GIRL NAMED MARIA

The bus drew up outside the luxurious but old-fashioned Grand Hotel Balkan in the center of Sofia, and I instructed the driver to wait with the passengers while I went in to find the guide who had been assigned to us by Balkantourist.

This hotel is one of the country's showpieces. The big chandeliers, marble pillars, wood panelling, and gilt-edged cornices are reminders of past graciousness and seem to indicate a desperate desire to keep up appearances, while diverting attention from the stained carpets and peeling brown paintwork. Uniformed waiters and footmen add a further touch of glamour. Once, when one of our visits had coincided with an International Congress of the Communist Party held here in the capital of hard-line Bulgaria, I had seen some members of the British Communist party staying at this hotel as visiting delegates. Today there seemed to be no lack of stout party officials and their even stouter women in badly fitting, shapeless clothes, eating or drinking in the restaurant. I could not help remarking the difference between these overpaid and overfed protagonists of the classless society and the poor peasants I had seen earlier working in the fields, or the women who work through the night to sweep the streets.

Our interpreter was waiting by the desk in the main entrance hall. She was small, dark, and rather attractive, with tip-tilted nose and warm smile which somehow did not fit in with my concept of the dedicated Communist ideologist.

She shook hands and introduced herself: "My name is Maria," adding an unpronounceable surname.

Maria at once became a firm favorite with the passengers. She was very young, just twenty-one, she told us, and recently married to a lawyer. She spoke excellent English, having studied it at the university. It was her job to show us the various historic sites in Sofia, then point out other places of interest on our route across the country, staying with us until we reached the border — all part of an organized plan to glorify the achievements of this "people's democracy." In addition, she was supposed to make certain that we did not stray from the recognized tourist routes and view some of the less perfect aspects of the "workers' paradise."

We toured the sights of the city, then continued our journey through the countryside. From time to time, Maria paused in her commentary long enough for me to question her on various points of interest, and sometimes to contrive to turn the conversation to my own personal relationship with Christ. Though educated in atheism, she nevertheless evinced some interest as I tried to show the relevance of Christ to her need in a Communist society. I was surprised and delighted when, at the end of the journey, before leaving us at the Turkish border, she asked me if I could get her a Bible. I had only an English King James Version with me, but this I gladly gave her, extracting a promise from her in return that she would arrange especially with Balkantourist to be our guide on the return journey in a few days' time.

Ten days later I returned, for our buses were now operating a shuttle service to and from Israel via Syria and Jordan. The party which we had taken out would return by ship from Haifa at the end of their tour, while the group we were bringing back had entered Israel at Haifa, completed their tour of the Holy Land, and were now travelling home by the overland route. It was not possible to make a two-way land crossing of the Jordan-Israel frontier. I found the operation a thrilling experience, especially as officially it was not possible to use Syria as a corridor for travel to Israel. However, we had been operating this route successfully for some years. It took a combination of faith, cheek, and a bit of business enterprise thrown in. As I was subsequently to realize, it was God's training ground for what lay in front of me. For it became through those years a "school of faith," to build the foundations of my belief in the greatness of God, His extreme faithfulness, and His power to overcome every obstacle. Those years brought me so close to Him that I never doubted Him or His ability in the face of the seemingly impossible. As Cyril Williams, one of our passengers, was fond of reminding me, "With God, difficulties can be overcome immediately, but the impossible takes a little longer."

Maria was waiting for us at the border as arranged. As soon as a suitable opportunity arose I continued our previous conversation. "Tell me, how are you getting on with reading the Bible I gave you?"

"Oh," she replied, "unfortunately since you were last here I have had a party of tourists every day. We get so little free time. This is the busy holiday season and we work from early morning until late at night. I have not had much time for reading. All I had managed so far is the Gospels of Matthew, Mark, and halfway through Luke."

I was thrilled. This was wonderful, far more than I had dared to hope. From the way she talked and discussed what she had read it was evident she was really interested. In the course of our last conversation before I left Bulgaria, she told me she was finding it difficult to understand the old English of the Bible I had given her. Would it be possible for me to get her a copy in her own language?

"Can't you get one here?" I asked, surprised.

"Oh, no," she replied. "It is impossible to obtain a Bible here in Bulgaria."

Naturally I promised to bring her one. Before we parted, we arranged that she would once again try to fix things so that she would be our guide on the next trip. This might be difficult, as guides were not supposed to work with the same people too often.

I had only three days in England before setting out once more. A quick call to the British and Foreign Bible Society in London produced six copies of the Bible in Bulgarian, which were delivered to my office just in time for the next journey. We encountered no specific problems at the Bulgarian border, and it was only after we had crossed into the country that I remembered the Bibles were lying openly in the back window of the bus, just wrapped in brown paper.

Maria met us at the usual place inside the Grand Hotel Balkan. I had no opportunity to speak to her privately until we reached Plovdiv, where we were booked to stay at the new skyscraper hotel Maritsa. After dinner, as she and I stayed talking, discussing the arrangements for the following day, I cautiously introduced the subject. "About that Bible. . . . "

"Oh, yes," she replied, too quickly, "I know what you are going to say. You could not get a Bible in Bulgarian, or you were too busy and simply forgot." The haste with which the words came out, together with a note of impatience in her voice, seemed to indicate a more than ordinary disappointment. If there had been any question in my mind as to her sincerity and her wish to have the book, this was quite dispelled, both by what she had just said and by the way the conversation developed. Clearly, here was no informer trying to trap me into a compromising situation, but a genuine seeker after spiritual truth.

"How many would you like?" I asked her.

She looked at me with some astonishment. "Well, as a matter of fact I was talking to my sister, and she would like one, and four of the other guides also said they would like a copy for themselves."

Six copies! By a wonderful coincidence it was exactly the number I had obtained from the Bible Society. When I handed them over, her face was radiant with delight.

Before we left our charming guide the following day, I tried to ask her whether she ever listened to the Christian radio broadcasts which are beamed regularly into Bulgaria from the West. At first she denied any knowledge of them, explaining that it was against the law to listen to any Western program. She was obviously afraid, even of the passengers on the bus, some of whom might have overheard her reply, for she kept looking anxiously around as we spoke. Seeing this, I waited until at one of our refreshment stops I could get her alone. She still looked a little worried when I repeated the question, but seeing that there was no one else within earshot she quickly confided that she tried to listen to the program as often as possible. "That was why I wanted so much to have a Bible," she confessed.

At the border we bade Maria a cheerful good-bye, expecting that we would meet her on the return journey, but we never saw her again.

Already we were a little worried by political rumblings in the Middle East. The area was in a state of unrest and everyone was uneasy about the situation. By the time we reached Istanbul, things had deteriorated sufficiently for us to check with the British consul whether we should continue our journey or return home. Reassured, we resumed our schedule and the long drive across Turkey.

Only later did we find out that, just thirty minutes after we had left the consulate, instructions were received to stop us as the outbreak of hostilities seemed imminent. The orders sent out by the embassy staff never did reach us, though they were supposed to have chased us all across Turkey. So it was that, in all ignorance of the situation, we rolled on through Syria into Jordan and finally arrived in Jerusalem. We received an enthusiastic welcome, although we were not expected since both our Jordanian representative and the consul had told the hotel that we were not coming. By now we were the only British tourists left in Jordan. We stayed just four days, into which we crammed as much hectic sightseeing as we could before being very sternly ordered out of the country by the consul, who was afraid for our safety. In company with our other group, who had been on the other side of the border and so on the other side of the war, we hastily evacuated when we found that the final emergency measures were being taken by the Jordan government. This was on June 4, 1967.

We left in a hurry, just before the actual fighting started. Both groups were safe, but our hasty return meant that we failed to keep our appointment with Maria. All we could do now was leave her in God's hand.

This was my first small experience of the hunger of those behind the Iron Curtain for the Bibles which it seemed it was impossible for them to obtain. I felt I ought to do something about it, and began to ask God to show me how.

4

CHRISTIANS SPEAK OUT

The envelope with the Yugoslavian stamp did not arouse any strong curiosity. I frequently had letters from eastern Europe these days, usually on business matters, occasionally from contacts and friends I had made in the course of my travels. So I slipped the letter to the bottom of the pile to take its turn.

When I opened it, I found it was from Pastor G. in a certain town, a man whom I had met once and to whom I had taken a liking, inviting me to preach at a service in his church. Since it was near the Hungarian border, several believers from that country were also expected to attend. He had already applied for and received the necessary permit from the police, and he hoped very much that I would come. The invitation was for May 1.

Although it was rather short notice, I knew this was an opportunity I must not miss. I arranged for an interpreter to come with me, and obtained as many Bibles as we could conveniently carry in the car, as well as supplies of used clothing. We knew that many of the Christians in Communist countries were desperately poor, since they are usually unable to get any work other than the most menial jobs, and if any of them are imprisoned, as many have been for their faith, their families can obtain no help from the state.

Here was an unexpected answer to my prayers. I had

been asking God to show me how I could help my oppressed fellow believers, and now He was offering me an opportunity. On the face of it, it might seem a long way to go just to preach a sermon, but I felt it was the next logical step.

We arrived at our destination fairly late on the evening of April 30 and found the pastor's house without difficulty. He was more fortunate than the rest of his congregation, in that he had an administrative job in one of the local factories, which enabled him to live in a reasonably modern house. Although he was in charge of the largest church in the area, and accepted as the most senior minister, he, like all his brother ministers, had to follow a secular occupation since the churches were too poor to support them financially. His problem was that his job caused some of the believers to treat him with suspicion — normally a man could not hold such an important position unless he was a member of the Communist party. He assured us he was not, but that the job was itself an answer to a prayer.

"Shall I call you at six o'clock tomorrow morning?" our host asked casually as we prepared to go to bed.

We exchanged dismayed glances. We had been travelling for two days and were very tired.

"I can make it earlier if you like," he assured us, cheerfully. "The service itself doesn't begin until eight o'clock, but people will be gathering for prayer from before six."

By the time we got there, at eight o'clock, the small building was already packed to the doors. Around three hundred people were seated on narrow, backless benches, so close together that there was hardly space to move, with many more crowded on to the platform, so that I literally had to climb over them to find a place to sit down with my interpreter. Soon every conceivable place was filled, even to the doors and windows, anywhere they could crowd to look and listen.

To these happy, warmhearted people, time seemed no object. The day was a public holiday, and they were spending it doing the thing they liked most — pouring out their hearts in worship to God and in warm fellowship with their fellow believers. The service, though ordered, was informal. Several Hungarian believers had managed to cross the border, news of the visit from an English pastor having spread by means of the efficient communications network which seems to exist between these groups of believers. Their presence meant that the entire proceedings had to be conducted in three different languages.

I was most impressed by the number of young people present, who not only sang vigorously, but contributed greatly to the service by performing with considerable talent on various musical instruments. It was when one of them stood up to tell what had happened to him when he became a Christian that I realized what lay beneath the surface, hidden under the warmth and joy of their very real and practical faith. Here was a hard core of suffering almost unknown to us in the West.

Hans was about twenty-one years of age, and had recently been converted in one of the services. I listened carefully as the interpreter beside me translated what he was saying. Hans told us how he had returned home that night, thrilled by the joy and peace which flooded his heart now that he had surrendered his life to Christ. As he walked in the door, the first person he met was his elder brother, an atheist and a member of the Communist party. Overflowing with happiness, Hans tried to explain what had happened to him, but his brother only turned on him angrily, demanding that he give up all this religious nonsense at once. When he refused, his brother in a violent temper pulled out a pistol, threatening to shoot him unless he immediately retracted.

Tears streamed down Hans's face as he told us his story. "What could I do?" he asked. "How could I stop being a Christian when it meant so much to me?"

Several of the rest of us were crying, too.

"I didn't know what to do," he went on, simply. "I hesitated for a moment, then said to my brother, 'Kill me if you must, then, for if you do I will go straight to be with my Jesus in heaven.' "

Hans watched almost paralyzed with terror as his brother's finger tightened on the trigger — then his wrist slowly dropped and, ashamed, he put the gun away. We shared the thrill in Hans's voice as he told us that this brother was now also a believer.

One by one, others of the young people then stood up, with similar stories of what it had cost them to confess their faith, how they were persecuted by their families as well as by their colleagues and teachers in school and college. After the service had continued for some time, a break was announced and everyone was served with food and delicious lemon tea before crowding back into the church building to continue the worship. Later on, when I had finished speaking to them, I was about to suggest another break, but as soon as I sat down I noticed many of the congregation pushing their way through the packed rows to the front. I asked the interpreter what was happening. He told me that they simply wanted to commit themselves to Christ; that despite all they had heard about persecution, they still wanted to accept the faith and make a public declaration of their identification with Christ.

Among them an elderly man particularly caught my attention. The interpreter whispered that he was the father of another young pastor who stood on my left, weeping tears of joy. Later I learned that he had been praying many years for his father, and now at last he was witnessing the answer.

How can I ever forget that day? I had heard stories about Christians in eastern Europe, but to actually witness such real faith in the midst of all the persecution and opposition was a shattering revelation to me. I learned for the first time that day what I was to find increasingly over the next months and years, that these Christians, for all their material poverty, have something far more precious to give us than anything we could ever give them. Their radiant faith, love, and fellowship, the depths at which they shared one another's sorrows as well as the joys, went beyond anything I had ever encountered in my own country for all its vaunted freedom. From now on, I would always return home from my visits to eastern Europe infinitely richer than when I left.

The service drew to a close. It was by now six o'clock in the evening, and most of the people had been there since early morning. I was taken on to another church only a few miles away where the service continued until ten o'clock that night, and then most of the people found places to sleep either in the church itself or in nearby homes, for they were to stay overnight so that the services could continue the next day as well.

After the services I was asked so many times for Bibles that the few I had brought were gone almost immediately. The Hungarians particularly asked for some small ones which they could hide in their clothes so that they could take them back over the frontier and past the police patrols. I simply could not supply enough. They begged me to come again, bringing more, since it was impossible to obtain them in their own country. Eventually I left with orders for more than I could hope to bring.

Although permission had apparently only been given

for me to preach at the one service, I ended up by speaking in several different centers in this area before I returned to England. Thus I was able to meet a great many people and get to know about their problems firsthand. This only strengthened my resolve to return, and to continue to help these people who were my brothers and sisters, even to the extent of involving my travel company and the staff, if they were willing. It seemed obvious to me that, with a fleet of buses continually visiting these countries, I had a perfect set up for transporting Bibles and other supplies. Was this what God had intended for me all the time? Possibly. In any case, the opportunity was there and the logical thing was to take it. No one can ever suggest that I was influenced by others, or that my subsequent actions were based merely on other people's suggestions. I had personally met these desperately needy Christians, and they had made known to me their needs and the best ways in which I could help them.

If I had any hesitation at all about returning, the touching farewell from the young people of that first church made the matter quite plain. "We prayed for you to come," they said, "and you came. Now we shall go on praying that you will come again, and you will come."

How could I answer that? I knew that their prayers carried more weight than all my petty protests of business ties and responsibilities. I did go back. In front of me as I write this is a letter from that same Pastor G., which arrived just two days ago. "We remember the blessings of your first visit," he writes. So do I. I have been back to that church several times, but nothing can ever eradicate the memory of those wonderful days which were so drastically to change my future plans, and eventually even to bring me to share their experience of testing faith.

5

RENDEZVOUS IN BELGRADE

I had a phone call one day from a friend, another David, from London who shares my concern for the Christians of eastern Europe. He told me of a plan to visit Hungary with a group of young Christians. Would I care to join them? It so happened that I had been wanting for some time to visit a group of believers in that country, and we agreed to cooperate. Since I was exceptionally busy at the time, we decided after some discussion that they would go on ahead, and I would fly out and meet them later.

I now had a problem. As I was not taking my own vehicle, how could I transport enough Bibles? The obvious solution was to use one of the buses. We had one making a scheduled run at the right time, and since it was still early in the season we could reckon that it would not be full of passengers. Rather anxiously I asked one of my regular drivers, Robert, to assist me. Robert is a Christian and knew what I had in mind, and after a little prompting he agreed. I arranged that he would travel with the bus as spare driver, in addition to the normal crew of two. Then, when the Bibles were unloaded, he would stay with them until we arrived to pick them up.

The plan seemed simple enough. Several hundred Bibles in cardboard boxes were loaded into the luggage trunk, along with several boxes of clothing for relief work. The bus was due in Belgrade about 1:00 P.M. on Sunday.

David and I, who would meanwhile have been visiting a church just over the Hungarian border, would rendezvous with Robert and pick up the boxes while the bus went on its way to Greece.

Unfortunately, the service we were at ended later than expected and the journey was longer than we had reckoned. As a result, it must have been nearly three o'clock when we finally made it to Belgrade, only to find that the bus, which in any case had been running ahead of schedule, had, without waiting, unceremoniously dumped Robert and the boxes in the big square outside Belgrade's main railway station. By the time we arrived, Robert's complexion was changing from white to green as he sat surrounded by milling crowds of people and police, his imagination working overtime. He had just convinced himself that we were not coming and was wondering how to explain away several hundred Bibles in various languages. He knew no one in Yugoslavia, and had no idea how to contact either us or our friends in Hungary or Rumania who could have taken the Bibles.

We hastily distributed as many boxes as we could to our contacts who were helping to get the literature over the borders to its various destinations, before ourselves crossing back into Hungary with our precious load. In those days we did not know what to expect at the borders, and although the Bibles were not in sight when we crossed over, the police, searching, came within literally a coat's thickness of finding them. Only the mercy of God spared us on that occasion.

The most memorable event on that particular journey was a meeting with a man who had asked for Bibles in Russian. He told us that near where he lived there was a big Russian army camp, part of the total 300,000 Russian occupation troops which it was believed were then in the country. Despite the danger, he was giving out Bibles to the soldiers. I tried to protest that he would be arrested and put in prison, but he merely shrugged his shoulders. He committed himself to Christ, he said, and if he was arrested, then there were plenty of others willing to carry on the task.

After he had stowed away the Bibles he took us outside and showed us his car. This amazing contraption was then thirty-six years old, and its condition was simply unbelievable. The bodywork was remarkably held together by metal sections that had been welded into the original frame; spare parts that were otherwise unobtainable had been handmade out of any scrap metal available; headlights balanced precariously on fenders that themselves looked ready to fall off; the doors, in order to stay shut, had to be fastened with string. I seriously doubted whether such an extraordinary vehicle would even get one hundred yards down the road without a liberal application of chewing gum to its more vital parts!

We held our breath with amazement as we gazed at this last vestige of faith, hope, and charity, whose more obvious failings were covered by a gleaming coat of deceptive red paint, and listened to tales of its exploits. We heard, incredulously, that in it the whole family dared to venture over the borders into Russia itself. The bald spare tire was taken off and the inner tube removed so that the whole cover could be stuffed with Bibles before being replaced. Side panels, which were so obviously only held in place by much welding, were opened and filled with Bibles before being painstakingly rewelded, and every nook and cranny was filled with more of the precious books. Its owner stood by proudly as we admired his handiwork, then begged us to bring him more Bibles for his missionary enterprise. We left him everything we could, with our solemn promise to return.

On this same journey I met another believer who had

suffered a great deal for his faith. In his desire to evangelize, he had invited some young people to his home to tell them about Christ and to pray with them. Neighbors, always willing to spy and inform, called the police who took him away for questioning. After they had beaten him for daring to allow his home to be used for a prayer meeting, they left him bleeding on the floor. He was terrified of what might happen, as he had a wife and two young children. "We are not going to put you in prison," they shouted at him. "We are just going to teach you a lesson so that you will not be able to speak about God again." Then they kicked all his teeth in and sent him home. But that could not stop him taking every opportunity to tell the Good News of Christ to his friends and neighbors.

I met so many others like these. Sincere Christians who only wanted to serve God in the best way possible, but who as a result were hounded and persecuted, even tortured and imprisoned. It was evident that the Communists wanted to stamp out all evangelical drive and energy within the church, leaving only the dead formality which not only gave them no cause for concern, but in many ways aided them in their avowed purpose. Pure Marxism is atheistic not only in principle but in practice. Even in speaking to my fellow prisoners I saw how they had been taught from infancy that God is not real nor Christianity relevant in our twentieth century. Although the prisoners in my cell were opposed to communism politically and contrasted its repression with the freedom of thought and action allowed in the West, they had nevertheless imbibed much of its ideology and teaching, especially with regard to the decadence of the church. We had many arguments over this, with only a minority prepared to listen, let alone agree with my declaration that the Christian Gospel is the only liberation and salvation of man.

I was moved by the endurance of the believers, who did not ask or expect to be delivered from their terrible situation; all they asked was that we should not forget them. The things we took them were more than merely Bibles, clothes, and money. They were for these forgotten people a symbol of hope, a reminder that they were members of a larger family who cared for them and prayed for them. Over and over again, they begged me to keep coming, as though our visits were an arm reached down from heaven, keeping them in touch with an outside world which loved and cared.

It was the words of the young people in that first service which kept me going: "We know that you will come back because we shall go on praying until you do." These words would not leave me and I became more and more committed to helping them. I began to tell my friends that if I ever gave up the travel business I would become a missionary to Communist Europe rather than a minister in England again.

Every time I returned from one of these visits it was with the feeling that I had left my heart behind. But still I could not do enough; the big operation had yet to start.

6

"ALBERT" THE
BIBLE-CARRYING BUS

One warm day towards the end of October, I was in
London on business connected with my travel company.
This was always a busy time of year, settling final details
of plans for the next season, and preparing brochures and
advertising. Looking back, it is difficult to remember
whether it was by accident or design that I met an old
business acquaintance whom I had first gotten to know in
New York some time previously. We had struck up a
friendship which was more than the casual business relationship, since we shared in common a vital Christian
faith, and we had been able to help each other in many
ways.

He knew a little about my involvements in eastern
Europe, and sympathized with what I was doing. Even so,
when he suggested that I might like to meet some friends
of his who could be useful to me, it was bus tours rather
than Bibles that I had in mind. I called that evening at a
flat in a residential area in west London. It was only when
I had entered and was introduced to the assembled company that I discovered the reason for the vagueness of his
words. There were four people present, including an
American whose face seemed faintly familiar. While I was
speculating about the significance of the meeting and why
I had been invited, my friend said:

"David, I'd like you to meet Joe Bass, the president of Underground Evangelism. They're very active in Christian work behind the Iron Curtain, and have been since 1960."

Suddenly everything clicked into place. This could be God's answer to my problem. I had been having difficulty in obtaining all the Bibles and New Testaments I needed to meet the requests of my friends in Communist countries. The societies from whom I had been receiving the literature had informed me that they could not supply the numbers I was asking for. Perhaps Underground Evangelism could help.

I launched into an account of what I had done so far, explaining how Crusader Tours was a perfect framework for this type of ministry. It was established as a registered travel agency, and our buses travelled regularly and frequently to Communist countries. Why not use these facilities to mount the biggest project ever. . . . My mind was running away from my tongue, and I had to pause to put my thoughts into shape. Why not build a special compartment into one of the buses, so that as the couriers came out with the news of the believers' needs we could transport to order whatever was requested? It was a mind-boggling idea . . . several thousand Bibles each trip . . . a special organization to handle the unloading on the other side . . . and teams to work with me . . . organization both to store and to distribute the literature . . . and most of all, someone who would supply all the thousands of Bibles, New Testaments, Gospels, hymnbooks, and good Christian literature for which we were constantly being asked. It was too big a project for me to handle alone. I had no financial backing, I could not afford to buy so many Bibles, and the poor believers could not afford to pay for them.

Mr. Bass responded immediately. Underground Evangelism knew the need and had been doing this very work for many years. He said they would supply all the Bibles we needed, as well as funds and some key people to help plan and carry out the work. We could cooperate with one of their existing teams already well established behind the Iron Curtain — in addition to my own contacts there were people on the other side who could be called in to consolidate the whole operation.

I needed no further encouragement. This was it, the answer to my prayers! I had been asking God not just to show me the way but at the same time to open the doors. This was surely what He had been training me for all these years. It was only the beginning, but my mind was already racing ahead, foreseeing the snags, making plans.

In the train on my way home that night, I was totally absorbed in the practical problems. The next day I went to look at the buses. I needed to find a way of constructing a compartment that would escape detection, yet be sufficiently large to carry enough Bibles to make the operation feasible. Not only must the compartment be hidden, but it must also be of easy access, for when we got the Bibles to their destination it would be necessary to unload them as swiftly as possible. Even with everything in our favor it would still take a long time to shift a few thousand books, and during this period we would be most vulnerable. Besides the risk of being seen by chance passersby, the vehicle would be virtually immobilized and we could not hope to make a quick getaway if danger threatened. Most important of all, the local believers who were involved must not be compromised.

Most of the obvious hiding places, such as a false floor, were ruled out immediately by the design of the vehicles which had an underfloor engine situated in the middle with access trapdoors along the central aisle of the bus. The border guards always looked at these first. Several small compartments located in such places as the air ventilation system or the front panels housing the electrical system were also out, as again these were too obvious. The final choice was based on all my experience of previous crossings and observations of the methods used by the guards. Though not absolutely foolproof, it should remain undetected by all but the most determined searchers.

Though our Bibles were hidden, we were not "smuggling" them across. I know this word had been frequently used, but I want to clarify it. It is not hairsplitting. There is a very real difference.

As I have said, there are no laws forbidding Bibles to be taken into these countries. One cannot break a law which does not exist. On the contrary, the constitutions of these countries guarantee full religious freedom to every citizen. And how can there be religious freedom without the Bible necessary? Thus they are breaking their own highest law, constitutional law, by illegally denying their people Bibles.

Why, then, did we hide the Bibles? For the same reason that a man travelling in a risky area keeps his money safely tucked away. Money isn't illegal. But because it is valuable he wants to protect it from being illegally taken from him. The Bibles we took were not illegal. No law banned them; the law implicitly permitted them. Some of the countries even dared to print Bibles, though this was chiefly for propaganda purposes. Our Bibles were valuable and we didn't want them taken from us by border guards violating their own laws. They were the law breakers, not we.

If, however, any country were to pass such a law, we would face the age-old question of obedience to man or to God. The disciples faced this question, as did the early Church, who kept the faith alive in the catacombs of Rome. And the believers of the persecuted church are confronted with the same dilemma today. Often the official churches are closed, or the nearest one is too far away. This leaves them with two choices: to obey man and not meet and not worship God, or to obey God and meet in illegal "unregistered" churches in houses. Their reply is that of the disciples in Acts chapter five, who, when forbidden to teach or preach of Jesus as the Christ, replied, "We ought to obey God rather than men." They are law-abiding people; they believe in obeying man's laws, until in doing so they have to disobey God. When it comes to a choice, they must obey God.

As I set about constructing the hidden compartment, I reflected that Britain itself, which has sent missionaries all around the world, first received the Scriptures when William Tyndale's Bibles were smuggled into England in the sixteenth century — in bales of wool and cloth, in barrels, and in sacks of flour. Despite every effort to stop them, the Bibles arrived and were distributed throughout the country. Tyndale was eventually arrested in 1536 and strangled at the stake, his body burned to ashes. Because of his obedience, the English people received God's Word.

So, in our work, we were prepared if necessary to follow the pattern of the first disciples; of the early Church; of those who brought the Bible to England — the pattern of the persecuted church of today.

Within a short time the first message came through from Joe Bass. Would we make our first crossing in December to deliver a special consignment to the believers in Rumania in time for Christmas? Having satisfied ourselves that we had done all that we could to the bus, we set off. I had selected one of our AEC buses which we had had built specially. It was just over a year old and well tested for reliability, though not the newest in our small fleet. A new one might have been too conspicuous, and there was the risk that an older one might break down. We code-named the bus "Albert" so we could communicate about it over the phone or by letter.

There were only three of us on the bus, Robert, Eric, and myself. We aimed to travel fast and light, so agreed to share the driving equally between us, thus being able to cover the long journey in the minimum time. I think we were all a bit scared of the prospect, and just wanted to get it over and be back home as quickly as possible. We drove from Dewsbury to Dover, took the overnight ferry to Belgium, then drove to our first stop in Frankfurt where we had been instructed to receive our load from the Underground Evangelism depot.

Having parked "Albert" in a side street, I went down the road to find a car-rental firm from which I rented a Volkswagen truck. We dared not take the bus directly to the depot. So we drove up in the Volkswagen, presented our identification papers, and collected as many parcels of Bibles as we could load into the truck. As we loaded it, the Volkswagen began to sink down to its knees — books are heavier than you think. Keeping careful count, since receipts had to be given, we managed to pack into the secret compartment of "Albert" five thousand Rumanian Bibles before we were satisfied that there were enough.

After picking up further detailed instructions as to where and how we were to meet with our team of helpers, we returned the Volkswagen to the rental firm and set off southwards for Austria. The loading had been a strenuous three-hour job on top of a long drive, and we were naturally tired. Still, at that stage we were happy and contented, not realizing what was in store for us, so in high spirits we found a hotel for the night to get some rest before the next leg of the journey.

We drove on south into Austria. No time for sightseeing despite the beauty of the scenery, for we had a job to do. We drove into Vienna in the darkness of a winter evening, a city preparing for Christmas, with bright twinkling lights, gaily decorated shop windows, bustling shoppers laden with food and gifts, carols played over loudspeakers, church bells ringing. We couldn't help noticing the contrast the next day as we crossed the border to an atmosphere of drabness and gloom.

But first we had to make a rendezvous with "George" (his real name is best forgotten) outside one of Vienna's largest hotels. As we parked in good tourist fashion opposite the main doors, he recognized us at once by the bus and introduced himself with a wide smile. He piloted us out to a house in the suburbs where he was staying with his wife, and after a good meal we excitedly talked over the plans for the last stage of the operation.

It was the following morning, when we went to make a final check on our load, that we discovered a serious problem. In Frankfurt, when we had loaded up the Bibles, everything had seemed fine, but twenty-four hours and several hundred miles further on, things were not as we had expected. Technically, all we had to do was to put in the front section of the compartment, which had been carefully made to an exact fit, seal the whole thing, and complete the job with a bit of dirt and a few oily rags, so that the fastening was not visible. But the weight of the books (more than two tons deadweight as we later ascertained), combined with the bumping on the bad roads, had made the floor of the compartment sag so much that the front section would no longer fit. The situation was desperate. Even if we unloaded, there was no guarantee that the thing would go back into shape. There seemed to be only one quick solution, if it would work.

We hauled out the hydraulic jack which was used to lift the bus when changing a wheel, and which was capable of lifting more than three tons. Searching around, we found some large pieces of timber and, putting these on top of the jack, attempted the almost impossible task of lifting the floor, the steel angle-iron supports (which had buckled under the strain), and more than two tons of Bibles, in an effort to restore the compartment to its original shape.

"Right. This is where you watch and pray," said Robert as he began to operate the jack. Slowly but surely it started to go up, until to our infinite relief the floor temporarily resumed its original shape. Now at least we could fix the front panel which, when in place, supported the whole load and prevented further movement.

We offered up a prayer of thanks, before hastily finishing off the job of concealment by throwing in a lot of tools, spare parts, and dirty rags, thus turning the compartment into apparent extension of the engine compartment. We had found that all the continental buses had their engine at the rear, just where our tools and odds and ends suggested that ours was . . . but it wasn't. Unless five thousand Bibles provided the motive power? Perhaps there was more than a grain of truth in that! Anyone searching the vehicle would be diverted by the fact that we had a row of side luggage lockers just like all the other continental buses, specially built to our order and disguising the true position of the engine.

Of course we knew that it would not be possible to conceal this immense load forever. The operation from the beginning was based on the principle of working hard and fast, taking in the maximum possible load in the shortest possible time, right under the noses of the Communists. Knowing how thoroughly they could search any vehicle once their suspicions were aroused, fifty Bibles could have been discovered, let alone five thousand. We were always to work on the principle of taking them off guard by the simple audacity of the plan — and this worked far better, and for much longer, than I ever dared to expect. Rather than being surprised by the fact that we were eventually caught, I am amazed that we escaped so long.

All was now as secure as we could make it, so, making the final arrangements with the others in the group, we set off. Our first hurdle was the Hungarian frontier. A few miles short of the border post we stopped for a while, for prayer and a brief Bible reading before facing what might lie ahead.

The inevitable question — why were we travelling only three in a fifty-one-seater bus — we met with a prepared answer which was also quite true. We made it our policy never to lie whatever the situation. This would not be pleasing to the Lord, nor, if wisdom was used, was it ever necessary. Even if directly asked if we had Bibles, which very rarely happened, our reply was to simply invite them to see for themselves. So we told the frontier officials that we had not been on this particular route before, and we wanted to check out road conditions and hotels, so that we could start to bring tourists through. It was a good enough reason, and they were satisfied. The usual search passed without a hitch and we pulled away with relief. Two more borders to go. The search on the crossing out of Hungary some hours later was more rigorous; there was always the fear that someone might be trying to escape from the country.

Then over into Rumania, where we faced the toughest test. Everybody out, open up all the lockers, remove all inspection covers, peer underneath, and of course a thorough search of the rear luggage compartment. But our camouflage had been well done. They suspected nothing, and soon we were gruffly given permission to move away.

We spent that night at a town not far from the frontier which left us a long drive over the mountains to Bucharest the next day; but tired as we were, we thought it best to get some proper sleep. It was past ten at night.

We were off again at seven the next morning, a brisk,

cold day with no snow. Although it was December, winter had evidently not set in in these parts. Robert took the first spell of driving while Eric and I settled down to keep as warm as possible and generally keep him on course for the next town. All went well until we came to a steep pass, descending several hundred feet by a series of hairpin bends to where the road levelled off in the valley before us. The view was spectacular in the winter dawn light. Choosing the lowest of the six gears, Robert started off down the pass.

The first indication of trouble came a few moments later as we noticed that a truck coming up the hill was snaking badly, its rear wheels spinning crazily. I glanced at our speedometer — the needle was going up.

"Slow down!" I yelled at Robert.

Unnervingly, he glanced back at me while he wrestled with the steering. "I can't," he answered patiently. "I'm in first gear already, with the throttle closed, but . . . she's running away. . . . There's ice on the cobblestones. . . . If I brake . . . she'll go over the edge."

By this time we were within yards of the first of the sharp bends, a sheer cliff rising on our left, a sharp drop on our right. "Albert" was sliding faster every second. With two tons of deadweight at the rear, the thirty-six-foot vehicle was swinging from side to side like a tail wagging a dog. I had a fleeting vision of us lying in crumpled wreckage at the bottom of the valley, surrounded by five thousand Bibles.

Suddenly Eric flung open the door and jumped. For a second, I thought he had lost his nerve, then I saw he was holding the red plastic waste bin which always stood at the front of the bus, and was scooping up grit from the side of the road and throwing it under the wheels. Just in time, this took effect. Robert was able to gently apply the brakes until the vehicle came under control.

In this manner we negotiated the rest of the pass, Eric running in front of the bus all the way down, until we reached the bottom safely, much to our relief. Fortunately that was the last of our troubles, and as we came out of the mountains and ran down into the plain for the last stretch to Bucharest, it became much warmer, so that it was nicely on time that we drove through the city center to our rendezvous at one of the largest hotels. These East European cities have one good point, there are no traffic jams to delay the traveller in a hurry.

Almost as soon as we pulled up, George was there, smiling his greeting. Our reservation was booked in a much smaller and cheaper hotel in the next street, but for the purpose of our meeting we needed secrecy, and what place could be more private than the noisy dining room of this large hotel filled with the new elite of the Communist state? These men, who held the destiny of so many poor peasants in their hands, drowned themselves in the noise and the alcohol which seemed to abound so liberally in that room. Who would notice us as we mingled our laughter and our languages over the meal that night? It always seemed to me that when these Communist party members had to choose between food and alcohol or the dedication of their ideals, they would rather follow the dictates of their stomachs than their heads. Does not the Bible so aptly sum this up when it refers to those "whose God is their belly" (Philippians 3:19)?

Right under their noses we discussed our plans, and were introduced to a Rumanian who would be working with us, a believer who was taking enormous risks to distribute the Bibles. We fixed the timetable for the evening. Since the operation demanded the utmost secrecy, we must wait until the streets were relatively quiet, but not too late, or "Albert" would be conspicuous on the roads.

Just after 11:00 P.M. the bus slipped away from the front

of our hotel, following at a discreet distance a small van which contained another of the team members. Gradually we turned off all unwanted lights, then dimmed the remaining ones as we drove away in the darkness towards the outskirts of the city. Now only an occasional bus passed our way, no cars except the odd taxi came into view. Somewhere along the road a small car unobtrusively joined us, keeping just ahead of the van. Then in the gloom of a dark, moonless night, we turned the bus off the road into the woods and with the engine turned off coasted to a halt out of the sight of any passing pedestrians. Before we actually unloaded, we took out some tools including the jack to give the appearance, if anyone should come by, that we had broken down.

Now we stripped the panels from the compartment and cautiously began to transfer as many parcels as we could to the other two vehicles. After we had loaded as much as possible into the little car I went with it to help unload at the other end. This meant sitting on top of the Bibles as we went around by a devious route, calling at several homes. It was quite an experience, driving down little lanes, looking for homes known only to the driver, climbing over back garden fences, dropping to the ground when a dog started to howl, for fear it would set off the whole neighborhood, knocking on windows to rouse the men who had dozed off while waiting for us to call. Then, when the car was emptied, back to the bus where already they had another load in the van waiting for us.

Willing arms reaching out in the darkness to help carry the precious Bibles. The house with a shed at the bottom of the garden. Hurried consultation; yes, they would take as many as we could leave, the believers knew the house and would be calling the next day to distribute them one by one to those who lived farther away. This man waiting here had travelled over four hundred miles to meet me simply because the believers were expecting us; in his village they had so few Bibles every one was precious. He wanted as many as he could conceal in his case to carry on the train back home. He had travelled all day, waited up all night for us, then must travel back all the next day so that he could go straight to work. Two days and nights with no sleep, eight hundred miles return journey, simply for a few copies of this ordinary-looking book.

He was not the only one. One man put his arms around me and gave me a great bear hug. Neither of us could understand the few words we exchanged in the dark, but his tears were wet on my cheek, more eloquent than any words, more than enough thanks for our labors. I did not know their names, nor the addresses of their houses; they were my brothers and sisters, that was enough. I saw their poverty and need. During the night I went into one home, two small rooms for thirteen of them. I was tired and hungry, they offered me food but all they could give me was dry bread, and to wash it down a cup of cold water. They had nothing else. I looked round the room — bare walls, hardly any blankets on the beds, although it was December. The children were sound asleep all around us, their pathetically thin clothes neatly folded. There was no sign of shoes for their feet. I gathered that their father was in prison for his faith.

At last we returned to "Albert", tired but happy, and found that the last Bible had been cleared from the compartment. The others were trying to clear away the signs of our presence. When all was finished, we looked at each other; too late now to return to our hotel. We would go to the home of one of the believers in another district nearby, and stay for the hour or two that remained before the town would wake to the new day.

George came with us to interpret. I asked where the husband was, as only the wife greeted us, and was told that he, with the elder son, was taking away some Bibles to others whom we had not been able to reach. All through the night, quietly, efficiently, the books were being distributed or hidden away safely before the police could find them. I stretched out on a chair in the living room and with the others was soon fast asleep, completely exhausted by the night's events.

It was light when I awoke. I suppose that I must have slept for three hours because the lady of the house had gone to work and we were alone, until one of the other men came to fetch us for a late breakfast. We did not want to stay long. This was our first major drop and we were anxious to get out of the country as soon as possible in case any suspicions had been aroused. There were always informers waiting to give evidence of the slightest unusual occurrence.

So after breakfast we made our farewells, but though we were physically parting from these people I could not forget them. More than anything it was the simplicity of their gratitude that I remembered — their tears of joy; that bear hug in the dark; the warmth of a handshake when, with a torrent of words that I could not understand, they gripped my hand until I could almost feel the bones crack. Then there was the greatness of their faith. They expected us, they knew that we would come. Had they not asked God to send them Bibles? He would not fail them. Such childlike simplicity touched my heart. It was Christmas, and our gifts had brought God to them in a new way. This was their best Christmas present. For me, it was the most wonderful Christmas ever, for it seemed as if Christ Himself in company with the angelic choir had entered with us into these homes.

We had a long way to go, back over those treacherous roads, until we were clear of the borders. Only then could we be sure that we were not being followed by the secret police. All the way across the country we were arguing. What should we do about the secret compartment? Coming in, we had had the whole thing assembled and full. Now that it was empty, all the panels were simply lying on the floor of the luggage trunk, which by now had been restored to its original condition. But . . . if the same guards saw us going out, and the layout was different, questions would inevitably follow.

I was all for going out with the compartment as it was when we came in. Less suspicious, I thought. Not so the others. They thought it should be dismantled. When I gave in to them, we were left with the problem of the two big panels and the seals lying on the floor of the trunk. The more we argued, the nearer we got to the frontier. Eventually the others became too frightened to cross the border at all with these sections in, though some innocent-looking pieces of wood could not arouse any suspicion, I thought.

The whole thing came to a climax as we neared the border.

"How far away now?" one of them asked at last.

"Several miles yet, according to my map," I answered.

"Right," the others said. "Out those pieces go."

We pulled over to the side of the road, the trunk lid came up, the sections came out, and everything was thrown into a ditch just over the hedge. We all got back into the bus for the rest of the journey, rounded a corner, and to our utter amazement we saw directly in front of us the watchtowers and barbed wire that showed only too plainly that we had misread our map. We had discarded our telltale panels by almost throwing them at the soldiers!

I think the next hour was one of the most agonizing imaginable, until at last, with a smile the officer waved us out. It was a good thing it was cold that day, it gave an alternative explanation for the way our knees were knocking together!

It was a great relief to get home and I was pleased to see my family. But I haven't told them this story until now.

7

BIBLES FOR THE PERSECUTED CHURCH

Soon the Bible operation was running pretty smoothly. But there were a few memorable occasions when, through no fault of our own, things just did not go according to plan.

Like the journey we made one April. This was the so-called Seven Churches Tour, one of my favorites, which took in the sites of the seven churches mentioned in the Book of Revelation, all of them of course in modern Turkey. For this trip we were not using "Albert," but had hired a similar bus from another firm, since ours were all otherwise occupied. In spite of the fact that we had no secret compartment I decided that, since we were going through Bulgaria, I would go along as co-driver and make a delivery of about four thousand Bibles and New Testaments. These were simply wrapped in plain brown paper parcels and loaded into the luggage trunk, with the passengers' cases in front of them.

The first part of the journey went without a hitch. Our tours were well known by now, and the border officials did not bother us much. The trouble began in Sofia.

Our guide, who was new to us, was friendly. In fact, she was too friendly. Everywhere we went, Anna came too.

"For goodness' sake, shake her off," I muttered to Peter Harvey, who had come along to help me with the Bibles.

"I've tried," Peter almost wailed. "I tell you, that girl just doesn't know how to take a hint. I suggested she might like the evening off, or an early night, and all she says is that it is a pleasure to help visitors to her country."

"She's probably taken a fancy to you."

"More likely you," Peter retorted, glumly. "But the point is, what are we going to do?"

"What can we do?"

The time for our rendezvous came and went. Peter and I exchanged despairing glances. At last we gave up and went to bed.

Our program allowed us only one night in Bulgaria, and the return journey was planned on a different route. We would have no chance to unload the Bibles on this trip. We were burdened with them, across Turkey, into Greece, through Yugoslavia . . . I had a sudden thought. It so happened that Yugoslavia was at that time having a small-pox scare. This could give me the opportunity I needed. I prayed hard about the whole matter and gradually a plan materialized. The believers were urgently in need of the Bibles and we had never failed to make a delivery yet. Before leaving Sofia the next day, I had already made arrangements to reroute our return journey through Bulgaria, pleading the interests of the passengers, and had gotten a message to my contact, revising the date. As for the border crossings, we would have to rely on God to close the officials' eyes.

If there had been any other alternative, I could not think of one. I certainly had a problem, but that was nothing compared to what followed.

We had halted at the border for the usual checks, and the passengers were standing around, some buying souvenirs, others strong Turkish coffee. I walked over to one group, just as an earnest lady was saying to her friend, "What a pity we have not brought any Bibles with us. I was reading in the magazine of Underground Evangelism how Christians on holiday often take Bibles in their luggage when they visit Communist countries. It would be such a splendid opportunity, with a bus like this."

That was when I discovered the meaning of the expression "a cold sweat." I could feel it literally running down my back, with a tickling sensation. Hastily I launched myself into the conversation and contrived to change the subject. I don't to this day know what I said. If only she knew! I prayed no guards had overheard.

At the end of the tour we crossed from Greece into Bulgaria. The Bibles were barely disguised by now, the paper wrappings hanging off in tatters. I found myself praying urgently: "O God, close the eyes of the guards, don't let them even look for Bibles this time." As Mike drove slowly through the barrier and an officer came forward, I instantly recognized a man who had been unusually friendly the last time I had passed this way. I leaped from the bus, rushed up to him, and shook his hand warmly. He seemed to hesitate a moment. In fact I am sure he did not recognize me. But he nodded and smiled politely as I spoke of our last meeting, and waved us all into the office to wait. The formalities completed, my friend called me over to open up the lockers. I did so, chatting away all the time, clearly to his embarrassment and, I am sure in order to be rid of me as quickly as possible, he gave no more than a cursory glance before ordering me to close everything up again. He continued to look puzzled as we drove away.

After that everything went to a carefully prearranged plan. We briefed one of the younger passengers, a good-looking young man, to talk with our guide and keep her out of our way. She seemed pleased with his attentions, not noticing when Peter and I slipped away to get on with the job. The whole operation went smoothly. God had once again made a way for us.

The only near hitch came right at the end of the transfer, and mercifully I did not hear of it till the next morning. One of the cars helping us drove away, laden with Bibles which were only roughly covered by a blanket flung over the seat. Seeing a friend at the side of the road, the driver pulled over to speak to him. What he did not know was that he had stopped on a taxi stand. Within minutes a policeman appeared, giving our friend a few nasty moments until he made a hasty excuse and drove off as quickly as he could.

Sometimes we would get unexpected calls for a delivery run. This one came at the end of August, through a routine phone call from George. "Albert" was with a group on holiday in Austria at the time, his panels stripped out and stored in our garage. George insisted that the load was needed right away, no other bus was available, and we could not repeat what we had done in Bulgaria; we had to have "Albert." We always said that we were delivering to order, and this was an order. So . . . we obeyed.

As it happened, my brother Ken was in charge of the Austrian group, so I phoned him and arranged that Robert, who was driving, would bring "Albert" to meet me at Vienna airport. Ken would arrange alternative transport for the holiday group. I also enlisted the help of Will Dickerson, who had worked with me before.

Taking the panels to Heathrow airport in Will's car presented few problems, but how does one persuade the girl at the check-in desk that seven feet, six inches of steel angle iron, various aluminum lengths as well as three heavy pieces of wood panelling and yards of cloth covering, are a normal part of one's luggage? Anyway, how is a girl on the BEA staff supposed to respond to such a challenge in the rush hour? Does their training manual devote a section to dealing with the materials transported by Bible couriers? Fortunately we were late, so that, after an initial look of amazement, she efficiently called a porter and ordered him to take the lot to the waiting plane. It took me rather longer to satisfy the customs officers at Vienna than it did later to transport the completed compartment into Hungary.

Despite these difficulties we eventually got the bus into the Bible depot where we loaded up before joining George to make the final arrangements. Together we checked lists, confirmed distribution point, and cleared every detail of the operation. We had worked together as a team for a long time now and the whole success of the work depended on the mutual trust, cooperation, and understanding which existed between us.

As we checked, we discovered we had loaded a whole consignment of literature in the wrong language. Everything had to be taken out and rechecked, while new parcels were hastily collected from the depot. I was called away while this was happening, so was unable personally to supervise the reloading but, assured that everything was now complete, I watched as the unit was sealed and made ready for the journey.

We always travelled in more than one vehicle, the supporting team going separately so that if one of us were caught it would not involve the other. This meant adhering to a strict timetable for the rendezvous, but involved far less risk than sticking together throughout. We crossed into Hungary at Hegyeshalom. We had been through this crossing many times before; always we prayed first, and God had always undertaken for us. So while Robert, who was driving, opened up the lockers, Will and I remained inside the bus, quietly confident, until Robert suddenly poked his head through the door, whispered, "Pray hard," and disappeared again. I did not take him too seriously; Robert always was one to worry. Next thing he reappeared, climbed into the driving seat, and slumped over the wheel, his face a ghastly color.

A more senior officer arrived, and ordered me to open up the side lockers again. Up came the lid, the officer pointed to a box, and fished out a Bible. Horrified, I realized that in changing over the loads, six boxes each containing a hundred Rumanian Bibles had been overlooked.

The officers conferred for a few minutes then turned to me.

"You know it is not permitted to take these books into our country."

I agreed, weakly, not caring to argue or ask to see the law forbidding it, knowing they didn't care about such legal "niceties."

"I regret it will be necessary to refuse you admission." Pulling a rubber stamp out of his pocket, he solemnly cancelled the visa entry. I tried to plead with them; after all, the Bibles were in Rumanian, not Hungarian, but they were adamant. However, I watched them carefully; neither conferred with anyone else, they made no notes of their actions, simply watched us turn around and drive back towards Austria.

Now what? The support team was already inside, expecting to meet us. All the contacts had been arranged well in advance and this was a highly important delivery. Despondently we drove back to our center in Austria. I was really worried. Not only was this our first failure; it could mean that we would be suspect in the future.

We sat down to talk it over. I felt strongly that we ought to go back and make another attempt or we were finished, because we could not know whether or not real suspicions had been aroused. Will suggested that we should pray, so we did, quite clearly and definitely asking God for guidance. Then we discussed the whole matter as calmly as possible.

First we called in someone who had a rough knowledge of Hungarian to read the stamp on the visa. Apparently it only said CANCELLED. Nothing more. The next point was that no record had been taken of the bus's registration, nor any personal data. There was a strong chance that nothing at all had been officially noted. Further, both our support team and our contact were waiting for us. We prayed again. Then Will pulled out a Bible and began to read. Leaning over his shoulder, I read the opposite page. We stopped simultaneously and looked at each other. Will read out the verse in front of him: "Therefore thy gates shall be open continually; they shall not be shut day nor night" (Isaiah 60:11). Then I read from chapter 62 verse 10: "Go through, go through the gates."

This convinced me. I told Will that I felt I should make the attempt but that he could fly home if he wished.

"Not now," he said. "No guidance could be clearer than that. I'm coming with you."

"Robert?" He had, after all, had the worst of the last encounter.

"I'll come." We were all determined to go through with it.

We decided to make our next attempt at Rabafuzes, on the main road between Graz and Budapest. It was dark when we arrived. Before reaching the border, we had stopped and prayed very definitely that God would confirm His promise and "open the gates." We were subjected to very intensive questioning, but I had carefully and prayerfully prepared a reasonable explanation for our abortive attempt earlier in the day. I did not lie, but told only what was necessary, including the fact that we had someone to meet in Budapest.

For a long time I thought they were going to let us

through, then after more than an hour, which gave them plenty of time to check with our first point of entry, the officer came back, bringing our passports. Now followed more questioning, then seemingly a change of heart, for suddenly he took the passports back with him for another interminable delay, while we prayed that, whatever the outcome, it would be God's will. Now we saw, in the dim light, that the same officer was returning. Silently he handed back our passports, seeming to scrutinize each of us carefully as he did so. Then, with a brief word, he motioned us forward. We were in!

At the first sizeable town we came to we stopped for the night. As I examined my passport before going to bed, I found to my amazement that it bore, for the Rabafuzes post, an entry stamp, with a CANCELLED stamp on top of it, followed by a second entry stamp. We had actually been refused at the second border, and they had changed their minds! What had happened in that moment when the officer had faced us in the bus? Was it that God had inspired my answers, or had there been divine intervention? We shall never know. We only know that it was a miracle, and one exactly according to the promise that Will and I had both received, that we were to "go through the gates." All we had done was to be obedient to the command.

After our mission was completed, we thought it prudent not to return by either of the routes we had tried earlier, but to go via Yugoslavia. Before I set out on my next journey I took the precaution of asking the passport office to issue a new passport. They obligingly told me that provided I paid the fee I could change it as often as I wished. I felt a little happier the next time I crossed by the old familiar route. And I took the precaution of having a good load of passengers as a cover.

One of my more memorable trips happened the following Christmas. This time my wife had put her foot down and insisted, quite understandably, that I must not be away over Christmas itself. This meant delaying our departure until December 27, so it was New Year's Eve when we arrived and made our delivery in Rumania.

At first we wondered whether such a night, when all the revellers would be out until the early hours of the morning, would be a bad choice. However, as it turned out not only were most of the populace rather the worse for drink but so were the police.

This time I was without any of my regular drivers, and working with a completely new team of assistants. Fortunately, the journey passed without incident, and thousands more Bibles reached the Persecuted Church.

The same could not be said of another run, done soon afterwards. This time, to my relief, we were back with the experienced satellite team who were used to coping with crises. But none of us had ever met this particular obstacle before.

The site chosen for the transfer was approached by a bad country road, little more than a farm track in places, along which we crawled, lights out as was our custom, in the wake of our pilot vehicle, an ancient jalopy incapable of doing more than thirty miles an hour. Suddenly this leading car braked and, peering through the gloom, we could see that the road ahead was completely blocked by a thirty-foot trailer and its truck, over which several men were bending in a vain attempt to start the engine. I saw the driver of the leading car in our small convoy get out to see what was causing the holdup, and followed him. No exchange of conversation was necessary to sum up the seriousness of the situation. Obviously the battery was flat and from the weak glimmer of the lights, almost completely done for. Two brawny men were trying to turn the engine over by hand, but failed to make any impression on it; the thing was too big. Others from our vehicles joined us but even with all of us trying there was absolutely nothing we could do.

An hour went by. Time was precious. In a few hours it would be daylight and no Bible transfer could be made then. I was walking back past the trailer, deep in thought and prayer, when curiosity prompted me to take a closer look at it. As I approached it, to my horror a cylindrical black object was poked out from an aperture, pointing straight at me. A gun? I froze for what seemed an eternity. Then the object began to wiggle gently. My mind searched for an identification. Could it be . . . ? An elephant's trunk! I imagine this was the first time on record that a two-vehicle "Bible convoy" was ever held up by a travelling circus!

Late as we were, we had no alternative but to reverse the convoy back down the road and search for another place for the transfer. Those Bibles were soon on their way into the hands of the believers.

Always, in this work, our first concern was to protect the believers. Our security measures in this respect were elaborate and successful. That is why I was able to tell the Czech border police that I had no names of Czech believers. I took the Bibles, my co-workers had the contacts. It was an excellent system.

I calculate that in the course of our many trips, we delivered over 150,000 Bibles, New Testaments, hymnbooks, and other Christian literature, to people hitherto denied them. Their joy, their gratitude, their overwhelming love, never failed to move me deeply. Reports came of a spiritual awakening and of conversions in areas which had received Bibles only months previously. The Word of God was doing its work. But still, it was only a drop in the bucket. For a quarter of a century, these people had been deprived of Bibles. For every one delivered, they appealed for hundreds more. Rather than satisfying the need, those we took rekindled the hunger of people who had long given up hope of ever owning one. More appeals came in. We knew the risk was growing with each trip but, seeing the desperate need, we had to go on.

I am often asked why it is necessary to go on taking Bibles into eastern Europe in the light of reports that the situation is easing and that Bibles are now freely available.

This is simply a cruel propaganda hoax on the part of the Communists. Unfortunately, it takes in not only the gullible general public in the West, but also certain societies who, in their eagerness to see the situation improve, are unwisely ready to accept the unsubstantiated word of Communist-controlled bodies in eastern Europe. Eastern governments, sensitive to Western opinion, have always claimed to give religious freedom. So when, in the 1960s, the true situation about the Bible famine was revealed by Christians coming to the West, a highly skilled propaganda offensive was mounted.

Widely publicized negotiations about Bibles were held with certain organizations. There was much talk, but relatively few Bibles were actually printed. And those printed were kept strictly under the control of the Communist governments — or of their controlled agencies, the state-run churches. Almost never did the Bibles printed filter down to the average believers. When some were made available, it was only by registering their names that Christians could receive them; and these names then formed the basis of police lists identifying the believers and setting them up for confiscation of the Bibles and possible persecution in the future.

Deception was practiced on a large scale. One society representative told how he was impressed on being shown, when visiting a seminary, copies of the Bibles for which his organization had provided the paper. What he did not realize was that these large, pulpit-sized volumes were Orthodox Bibles, in the Rumanian language, placed on the desks of a Hungarian Protestant seminary! As soon as the important foreign visitor had left, they were quickly retrieved and locked away. We learned this from one of our friends who was there at the time, and subsequently came out to the free world.

Outside the capital cities, among ordinary believers as distinct from the official church leaders, we found a universal skepticism about the governments' claims that Bibles were officially and legally available. They were amazed. Ironically, people in far-off Australia and New Zealand have heard that Bibles are available in Rumania — but the Rumanian believers themselves have never heard of them — much less are able to get them!

Obviously, I am unable to go into great detail about the many methods which we developed, and which Underground Evangelism is still using, to get Bibles into Russia and other Communist lands. Some may wonder if I am giving too much away in this book, but in fact I have most carefully drawn the line as to what I can safely disclose.

As we gained experience, the most ingenious plan of all came gradually into our minds. As I studied the map of Europe, the plan began to take shape. I discussed it with the teams and we decided it was feasible. All that was involved was to offer special tours of eastern Europe, visiting various Communist countries in turn.

The first time we tried it, it worked perfectly. The tour travelled to Austria, where we loaded five thousand Bibles, before crossing into Hungary, where we unloaded. Then we turned south into Yugoslavia where we met our supply vehicles bringing us a load of Bulgarian Bibles which we transported into that country. This vastly increased the amount we could deliver on any one trip. We used this method several times without mishap so, going one further for June 1972, we planned the ultimate in Bible deliveries.

Still using the travel company as a base, but accepting advice from others in Underground Evangelism, we sent "Albert" to the bus builders to have new names painted on the illuminated signs and rear panels. By changing the name to Trans Europa Tours, it was suggested, we would avoid too many questions being asked. The tour left England on June 19, having been advertised on some hastily duplicated supplementary pages which we sent out with our travel brochure. It was destined to travel to Germany, where we would stop overnight at the Hotel Strauss in Wurzburg and load up with Bibles during the night. Next day it would cross into Czechoslovakia, spend two nights there while the Bibles were unloaded, cross into Austria to pick up more supplies, then travel through Hungary into Yugoslavia and finally into Rumania for the advertised destination on the Black Sea coast. The total loads which could be delivered in this one round trip would be something like 15,000 Bibles or 36,000 New Testaments.

Unfortunately, "Albert" was caught at the Czech frontier at the beginning of the most daring of all the Bible runs. For the moment it seemed that this was checkmate . . . but was it? Certainly it was Czech, but was it really the end of the game?

8

INSIDE BORY PRISON

God has an uncomfortable way of taking us at our word.
I had always prayed that I might be in the "front line" of
Christian service; now I was behind the lines, captured
and in prison. For so long I had seen the tremendous faith
of the believers under suffering; now I was to share it with
them. My cruel interrogator had condemned me to rot
and die in a cell.

As if to emphasize his threats, the door burst open and
I was taken out with my few meager belongings and
thrown into cell seventy-six farther down the corridor. So
this was prison life.

Locked in with four strangers in a small room six feet
wide and thirteen feet long, no bigger than an average
bathroom. On Saturdays and Sundays locked up for the
whole twenty-four hours, with Monday to Friday twenty
minutes' exercise allowed in a small yard. No privacy.
Every action performed in the presence of at least four
other men, with the ever-watchful eye of a guard staring
through the grille in the door. Smells. The odor of overcrowded bodies, the stench from the toilet in the corner,
overlaid with the reek of cheap cigarettes. The indefinable
prison odor of stale air and damp stone floors. At mealtimes the sickly, all-pervading aroma of bad food.

Night came. Five men with only four beds, the lights
burning incessantly, the heat, the stench. Still the

watching eye of the guard peering in, the sound of dogs howling under the walls, and the stamping of the feet of the armed patrols. Searchlights on the walls outside and guns at the ready. Maybe this is all a bad dream. I'll wake up tomorrow in a comfortable hotel room, breakfast waiting, the bus ready for the next stage of the journey. Or maybe at home, Zena with me, the girls' voices chattering in the next room. . . .

The sound of a key in the lock, a guard crashes in. Everybody up. He points to my boots, apparently left in the wrong position. I don't understand a word but one of the others, sensing the situation, silently moves them. More words in Czech, probably a warning, but to me unintelligible. As we settle back I try to pray, but words are difficult to find, thoughts hard to concentrate. Yet God was there. We were political prisoners, treated far worse than even criminals or murderers.

The buzzer sounds. It is six in the morning and time to get up. If we are not awake immediately a guard will be in. Wash in the cold water provided, fold the coarse blankets to an exact size, pile the rough beds together, then sweep and clean the cell. Just before seven the sounds of breakfast — chunks of bread being placed on a ledge outside the door, followed by battered aluminum cans. Next the sound of the big wheeled bins containing the revolting coffee substitute slowly pushed from cell to cell while a small portion is ladled into each can. A further pause, waiting for a guard to open the door briefly while our waiting hands grasp the dry black bread and drink. Hardly time to swallow what little there is before the door opens again for us to put the cans out.

Now there was nothing more but to sit on a hard wooden stool with metal studs for two or three hours until a senior officer came for cell inspection. This was when we could hand in letters, complain if we dared, or be punished for some small detail which was not correct in the cell. This was an extremely difficult moment for me, since I spoke no Czech and the officers no English.

Soon after inspection the buzzer would sound again for exercise. The area between two wings of the prison was divided into six sections, varying slightly in size from little bigger than our cell to nearly three times as large. In these still cramped spaces the inmates of two cells exercised together. An elevated wooden tower held an officer who supervised us to prevent any communication between the sections. Twenty minutes later, back to the cell to sit until the rattle of spoons being placed on the ledge outside the door heralded lunch. A further wait, then the soup trolley with its greasy bins would be heard as a ladle dispensed the water with bits of vegetable or macaroni which masqueraded as soup. The other prisoners usually poured it down the toilet. I suggested we should return it to the guards, but the others insisted that if we did, our rations would be reduced still further. Often the remainder of the meal would consist only of blackened, dried-up lentils or more macaroni.

The last meal of the day came at approximately four in the afternoon, and usually consisted of rice, commonly referred to as "Vietnam," since it was rumored that Czechoslovakia imported considerable quantities in exchange for the guns and ammuntion sent to the Vietcong rebels. Our problem was how to pick out the mouse droppings before eating it. Other days the meal would be just potato, or a kind of dry cake containing sunflower seeds. Four more hours of sitting on the same hard stools, then an eight o'clock buzzer meant that we could put down our beds. Another hour before the final buzzer went for silence. No more talking; we must settle as best we could in our cramped conditions for the uncertain terrors of the night.

Because of the gloom and the locked doors, our lives were ruled by a routine of sounds. Mealtimes were welcomed only for the break in the monotony, as were any other sounds which might herald some relief. Apart from mealtimes, the clatter of the key in the lock was dreaded. It could mean anything from a letter from home, the terrible interrogation room, molesting by the guards, or that a prisoner would disappear . . . not to return.

There were 2,500 of us in Bory prison, a gloomy building, 150 years old, built in the reign of Maria Theresa and badly in need of repair and renovation. Under Communist rule the chapel had been turned into a workshop. It was a maximum-security jail and while I was there they developed one of the eight wings into what the medical staff referred to as the "extermination block" for political prisoners. This held 500 of us, under interrogation and awaiting trial, some of whom could wait up to two years under such appalling and overcrowded conditions. Even the newspapers openly condemned the system under which 75 percent of the prisoners suffered severe mental and psychological collapse. The medical staff also criticized the terrible waste of Czech youth who must spend a minimum of three months awaiting trial, the conditions undermining their health for the rest of their lives.

The prison was surrounded by a twenty-foot-high wall with machine guns in towers. Inside there was a space between the wall and an electric inner fence, where prowled the dogs, reputedly half wolf, which guarded us day and night. Many times we discussed the possibility of escape, but it was clearly futile. Apparently one man had tried, succeeding in evading the fence and dogs before being shot by the machine-gunners. They brought back his bullet-ridden body as a warning to the others.

In my previous cell I had known companionship, although I had only been there for three days. Now I had to adjust again as I found myself abruptly taken from them and thrust in with strangers. At first there were only two others, until the cell filled up again with its usual quota of five. Hansa, the elder, was a forty-six-year-old Czech. His bald head, sallow skin, and bad teeth marked him as a regular inmate. I subsequently discovered that this had been his fourth unsuccessful attempt to escape from the country. His moods varied from the sullen and despairing to sublime comedy, depending on his hope of release.

The other prisoner, Vince, had also attempted to leave the country illegally, a political offense. Thirty years old, he had other things on his record. He was proud of his four-year-old son who now lived with his wife, from whom Vince was separated. Vince's first brush with the law had come about because he had been out drinking with a prostitute. As they came out of a café and waited at a bus stop, the woman vomited over him so that, disgusted, he pushed her into the gutter. An ambulance took her away and she was given treatment for drunkenness but no further examination. Four days later she died of a fractured skull, and Vince was sentenced for manslaughter.

It was then disclosed, by a doctor who was a friend of the family, that Vince himself had, not long before, received head injuries in an accident to a truck he was driving, and he was able to successfully plead diminished responsibility. Instead of five years in prison, he found himself sent for three years to a mental hospital. Here he lived in a large ward of one hundred men, some of whom were so unstable that they would eat their own excrement. The nurses who cleaned them up would then go on to prepare food without even washing their hands. Shocked and disgusted by these conditions, Vince escaped from the hospital and made his way to the border to flee the country, but he was caught and sent to Bory prison, charged under paragraph 109 of the penal code.

Despite his terrible background, Vince was fortunate in having the support of his family, who tried in every way to help him. We spent nearly five months together and he probably did more than anyone else to help me. We became good friends. In the early days when I could not understand the language and knew nothing of the rough prison routine, he did many little things for me. Those mornings when the dreaded buzzer would call us up to a new day and we had to strip our beds and fold the torn and filthy blankets into the exact shape and pattern dictated by the officers, it was Vince who would come over to me and patiently teach me, day after day, the quickest way to do it. I hope that God in His mercy will repay him, for I cannot.

The days passed slowly. I felt I was already a condemned man, found guilty without trial. I prayed for something to happen, and I am certain that others were praying, too. For a miracle did happen. On Friday, to my astonishment, the cell door opened and I was called back into the interrogation room for more questioning. This was to go on for another three months before they were finally satisfied, but at least they had opened the cell door, despite their threats.

They had various methods of extracting information, as I had plenty of opportunity to discover. In interrogation every possible trick was used to trap us into an admission of guilt. Other techniques were used also. Alex, a West German, was in on a serious political charge, and like me refused to talk. So the secret police wrote to his wife telling her that he had been having affairs with Czech women. This was untrue, but out of spite she wrote back giving the police full details of her husband's activities, which included attempts to smuggle several people out of Czechoslovakia. As a result, Alex was found guilty and sentenced to six years.

I received papers from the prosecutor indicating that I was being charged under paragraphs 100 and 124 of the penal code, which meant nothing to me. At the same time I was told that an attorney had been appointed to act for me, Judr. Karl Strejce of Pilsen. Although I had written to the British consul in Prague notifying him of my predicament, so far I had not been allowed to see him. Meanwhile the interrogation continued and on July 3, my twelfth day in prison, my attorney was allowed to come into the interrogation room and listen, though I was not allowed to speak to him, nor he to say anything, either to me or to the interrogators.

On July 12 I heard that I would be allowed a visit from the consul, Mr. McCallion.

I had waited anxiously for this, for here would be my opportunity to protest against my detention and find out what were the prospects of my release. I was allowed to change into my own clothes for the occasion. Already I had lost weight, but since they were a casual jacket and trousers, the loose fit did not show too much. My morale was rising as we marched across to the interrogation wing where the consul was waiting. Before we entered the room, the police interpreter took me on one side. There was just one thing, he told me. I was not to discuss anything relating to my arrest, my detention, or my "crimes." All I was allowed to talk about was my family and business affairs. This was an unexpected blow.

As it turned out, our interview was far from private. In the same room were two interpreters, the prosecutor, a girl stenographer, two police officers, and my interrogating police, besides the embassy interpreter. It would have been hopeless to try to talk about my immediate problems. The consul had brought me some English books as well as a parcel of food, and for these I was grateful, though in my bitter disappointment I may not have shown it. We talked of personal matters, but I had little heart even for this. At the end of half an hour the interview was brought to an end, and I was taken back to change into prison uniform and return to the cell. I was shocked, frustrated, depressed. I felt all hope was gone. Apparently even the British government was powerless to help me.

Still the interrogations went on, in an attempt to wear me down. One day I found all my belongings piled up in the interrogation room. My interrogator, a hard-faced young man, barely thirty, was ingratiating.

"You see we have your things here, Mr. Hathaway. I am sure you would like them back."

I said nothing.

"And we would like to give them back to you. All you need to do is tell us the truth, and we will let you go home. Now, tell me, to whom were you going to give the Bibles?"

Silence.

"Who gave you the Bibles?"

Silence.

"Do you have a depot or office in England? We only want to get the true picture, you understand. Then we will let you go."

I am glad I had the sense not to believe them. I later found out that this was a common trick to make prisoners confess, and so be given a longer sentence.

Another day: "All these Bibles were kept in your office at home, Mr. Hathaway?"

"They were not."

"We know you loaded them in England. Did you buy the Bibles yourself?"

"No."

"Who gave them to you?"

Silence.

"Perhaps you had better go back to your cell and think again."

A few days later, the same routine.

"Where did you get the Bibles?"

It was so wearying that after a while I was tempted to go along with them. Anything, if I could only get out!

Still that constant repetition: "Tell us what we ask, and everything will be all right, Mr. Hathaway."

I had been told that the interrogation would finish on August 15, but when I went to the interrogation room that day I found my two months' ordeal was not yet over.

"I am sorry, we must ask you some more questions."

At the end of the session I was presented with more papers in Czech to inform me that I was now being charged with another paragraph, 148, for contravening import-export regulations with regard to the Bibles. Wearily I went back to my cell. Would I have to go through the whole process yet again?

I met Brown Suit as I was being marched back along the corridor. We stood aside to let him pass. He gave me a sly grin. "*Five, nil,*" he remarked.

I did not appreciate the joke.

That night I was awakened in the early hours by a violent thunderstorm. All the lights had failed throughout the prison and we were for the first time in total darkness. I jumped up and tried to peer out of the little window; I could just manage this by climbing over the bed and hanging on by my fingertips. It was an extraordinary sight. The rain was sheeting down in torrents, and since all the floodlights were out, the guards were firing rocket flares. We could hear the bang, then see the glow in the sky. At the same time, other guards were operating battery-powered searchlights which they played over the walls. I tried to time the interval between the rockets, judging as best I could with no watch. By counting the seconds, I estimate there was one every two minutes. For the first time I was really aware of the formidable strength of the security surrounding the prison. I do not know whether I was more shocked or frightened, but certainly I realized as never before the impossibility of escape. I have memories too of other nights when I could not sleep and lay awake listening to the howling of the wolf-dogs outside the window.

How can I describe my feelings of utter despair at times like these? Alone, a thousand miles from home in an alien country, I could see no hope of ever being released. My thoughts were constantly with my wife and children at home. I prayed as never before.

Further problems arose on August 28. We were all moved down to a cell on the ground floor, number sixteen. This was worse than anything I had experienced, or even imagined, so far. Now there were no beds, just four filthy sacks stuffed with straw, stained and stinking from years of use. There was no longer a window; this one had been blocked up with glass bricks which prevented any circulation of air, though they let in a limited amount of gloomy light. Now, when the others smoked, and some were chain smokers, it was impossible to free the cell from the acrid smoke. As a nonsmoker, I found this intolerable. As if that were not enough, the cell was so damp that water ran down the walls, and the clothes we took off at night were almost too wet to wear the next day. It was appalling. In desperation I wrote a letter of protest to the consul.

The day after I wrote the letter, I decided that if I was going to ask the consul to help, then I must at least explain my cause to the prison authorities. I found someone who could translate for me and requested to see the *Ober Kommandant* of the prison. A little to my surprise, my request was granted within a few hours. They took me, with an interpreter, to the commandant's office where I put all my complaints: no ventilation, the cell damp with moisture, broken lavatory bowl, no beds, overcrowding. The commandant listened politely and asked me if that was all. He agreed that the cells were designed for only one or two persons, he agreed that we needed beds, but who was I to complain? I was a prisoner, nothing I could do would alter things. He knew the prison was overcrowded, but he would do nothing to help.

I might have known it. This was a Communist prison. So far as they were concerned, I was only a number, 10035, nothing more. Under communism a man is nothing; the state is everything. All else must be subservient to the supreme will of the state itself.

Was I discouraged? No, not really. I had at last done something positive. I had succeeded in presenting my case, and I had shown them that the British do not take things lying down. This was only a beginning. I had found a voice.

I also had something to look forward to. My interrogation was to finish on September 8, and I was to have a visit from my family, so the police informed me. Perhaps my wife and brothers? Surely Zena would come.

Once again I was taken to change into my own clothes, then over to the interrogation room for the final part of my statement to be completed. I was supposed to have all the material which had been taken down read over to me but there was no time. My family would be waiting for the visit. As a parting gesture, I was given another paper from the prosecutor, indicating that another paragraph had been added to my accusation.

With all this on my mind, I went to the visitors' room at the prison gate. Zena was not there! I had tried not to expect it too much, but I was bitterly disappointed that she had not been able to come. My twin brother Ken was there, with the consul, and I was pleased to see them. Shaken by the latest news of the further accusation, I poured out all my complaints about the terrible conditions, the disgusting cell. I pleaded with Ken to get me out, to *do* something. Surely they could do *something* to help.

Seeing me in this condition, Ken went home to take really seriously the task of trying to get me free. I only heard afterwards how upset he was. I realize now that it must have been a considerable shock to him.

9

PERSONALITIES IN PRISON

Throughout my time in prison, I refused to learn to speak Czech. However, several of my cellmates spoke German and as my knowledge of the language improved, I began to take part in conversations in the cell and the exercise yards. We also used to play chess when we could, or read what books we were allowed. These were all Communist propaganda, designed to reeducate us. There were only twelve books in English, and who wants to read 700 pages on the *History of the Chinese Revolution*?

I calculate that during my time in Bory I must have met more than a hundred people to speak to. I doubt if the authorities were aware of the extent of communication among us, or of how rapidly the latest news or prison rumors spread around. Regular conversations were held by means of tapping messages in Morse code on the cell wall. This infuriated the guards who did their best to stop it, but because it became too widespread, and also because of the echo, it was impossible to isolate and stop it completely.

Some of the prisoners were great characters, as were also some of the officers. One officer in particular I shall not easily forget. He was known to us as Dachel (little dachshund), since what he lacked in stature he made up for by the loudness of his voice. Dachel particularly took great pleasure in standing in the cell doorway making rude remarks about me in Czech, which the others obligingly translated after he had gone. One of his favorite comments was that Czechoslovakia did not need British tourists with their filthy British money, and he had some precise suggestions as to what we could do with our pound notes.

It was Dachel who brought the news that we were no longer to have pens, but must henceforth write our letters in pencil. He asked all the others in the cell to hand over their ballpoint pens. As he spoke in Czech, I refused to obey. My attitude was that he must ask me in English, which none of the officers could speak. I had not asked to stay in their prison. For two months after this the guards made periodic searches of the cell since they knew I had a pen. In fact I had two or three. I used to hide them in different places so that as fast as they discovered one I would replace it with another smuggled in from my family or the consul. This mental stimulation helped me and I still had two pens when I left the prison.

One officer at Bory was much more pleasant than the others. He was an older man who had possibly fought with the British during the war. Whatever the reason, he was kindly disposed towards me and offered to do what he could to make things easier for me, "because," as he said, "I don't want you to go back to England with a poor impression of our Czechoslovak prisons!" I am grateful to him for many little kindnesses he showed, both in the way he spoke to me and the privileges he was able to give me. Here at least was one officer who saw me as a human being and did not curse and swear at me for being a believer.

Probably my closest relationship in prison was with Hans, my cellmate for over three and a half months. Hans was a Catholic, though he had lost most of his faith by the time he came into my cell. No wonder, because he had already served a sentence of two years on a similar charge to mine, and as he walked out of the prison with a great sense of relief at the end of his sentence, he was rearrested, and charged with speaking against the régime while in prison and accused of not having been reeducated — or brainwashed. This was when I first knew him. He was completely shattered, mentally and physically, and his faith was almost gone. We had long talks about the Christian faith — he spoke English — and as a result of these conversations he began to turn to Christ for help and support. During the time we were together I saw a tremendous change in him, both in morale and spiritually. Even his sister commented on it when she came to visit him. It was a help to me to share my faith, but he in his turn insisted that I should have some of the extra food which was brought in for him by his sister.

Many of the prisoners were in the political cells because they tried to escape from the country. Their attempts were an unending topic of conversation. As they discussed the possibility of further ways of getting out I learned from them a great deal about the Communist borders and how they are guarded and patrolled. At the time they did not appreciate the reason for my intense interest.

Some of the stories were tragic. Stefan, who was brought into our cell for three days only, for the period of his trial, was only twenty years old. He had been a border guard and his unnecessarily elaborate escape attempt had ended in ignominious capture. Instead of making his attempt directly from his position on the border, he made careful preparations which included a bulletproof vest, metal shields on his arms and legs, pepper to deal with the dogs, and gasoline to confuse the scent. Then, having stolen his automatic rifle, he hijacked a car several miles from the border; but the driver, using the excuse of running out of gasoline, pulled into a garage and telephoned the police. He was arrested twenty miles from the border. Even in prison, Stefan could not resist boasting about his intention to make money out of his escape by selling to the West locations of Russian rocket sites in Czechoslovakia. Challenged by a cellmate to show where they were, he drew a sketch map which the other prisoner immediately handed over to a guard.

Stefan was in our cell during the time of his court-martial. His sentence was a total of fourteen years on twelve different accusations. That evening he was brought back to the cell in a daze, not yet able to comprehend the severity of his sentence. One of the other prisoners gave him some sleeping tablets, but still he moaned and groaned in his sleep all night. The next morning the police came to take him away.

Another cellmate was a Rumanian who was waiting to be sent back to his own country. He had stowed away on the top of a railway freight car leaving Bucharest for, as he thought, Yugoslavia and Austria. All he had with him was a plastic container of water and six bars of chocolate. Unfortunately for him, the train went by a different route through Hungary and Czechoslovakia. For six days in a cold November he lay in the open on top of the wagon, unable to move for fear of giving himself away to the police guards who watched the railway lines. Halfway through his ordeal, he dropped his waterbottle. He remained undetected until, a few miles from the German border, he was trembling so much from the cold that his foot knocked uncontrollably against the side of the wagon. The noise attracted a police dog which with a border guard had just passed by unsuspecting.

Perhaps the most to be pitied were those who had been caught trying to help their fiancées escape. It seemed to be a regular thing that young men who had East German girl friends did not try to bring them out directly from East into West Germany but preferred to go through Czechoslovakia. Escapers attempting to go directly to the West from East Germany were usually shot, whereas the Czech borders are mainly guarded by dogs and electric trip-wires, resulting in arrest rather than death. I remember one strong young German, arrested and brought into my cell, weeping brokenhearted at the knowledge that he would probably never see his girl again. It is personal tragedies like these which bring home the callous hard-heartedness of a totalitarian régime which puts politics above people and has no regard for personal feelings. I wrote in one of my letters to my wife (which the censor failed to pass), "There must be something wrong with this system which needs to close its borders and can only maintain power by holding people prisoner against their will." The system is so riddled with fear that it is afraid of free expression, free speech, or any form of individual liberty on the part of its people.

One of the more amusing boys I met had been arrested, not for trying to leave the country, but for trying to enter illegally. He was a West German who one night in a restaurant had become a little drunk and as the result of a bet over a bottle of whisky he agreed to break into Czechoslovakia and mail a card to prove his success before returning to the West. As his home was in a small town very close to the border, he thought this would be easily accomplished. Indeed, he had done it before. Unfortunately on this occasion he lost not only his bottle of whisky but his freedom, being caught in the process by the Czech police and sentenced to ten months for his offense.

I also met a boy of eighteen who had been given eight-een months for pulling down a Russian flag one night. I heard of a teen-age girl who had eight months for hitting a policeman — on what provocation one could guess. Others were awaiting trial on the major crime of being without work. Under the Communist system full employ-ment is promised and this is carried out in strange ways.

One way is to imprison anyone who is out of a job for more than a few weeks.

I was reminded of a comment by one of our guides in Bulgaria, who had told me of her country's boast that no family was without a home. They achieved this, she said cynically, by the simple expedient of housing whole families in one room and if more space was needed, by subdividing rooms with partitions, thus providing accommodation for two families.

A lawyer who was a prisoner told me that under the present régime in Czechoslovakia it is estimated that one person in every three will spend some time in prison in their lifetime, most of these on political grounds. When a man goes to prison the state makes no provision for his wife and family, who often must starve. This is a desperate problem for the families of believers who are imprisoned for their faith.

All prisoners must pay for their accommodation when on remand. This of course included me, and like all the others I was presented before my release with a bill for my stay. This was calculated at a rate of 20 Kcs per day from the day of my arrest until my final appeal in court, a total of 3,500 Kcs. In addition, the prisoner has to pay the expenses of the court. For this I was charged a total of 600 Kcs, then another 400 Kcs for the appeal. Finally, all prisoners must also pay the lawyer; there is a legal-aid system. My bill came to over $480 which my family had to remit through the British embassy in Prague. Czech prisoners who cannot pay are given special slips and the state deducts the amount owing in monthly installments from their wages. One prisoner who was with me finally left with debts of over 10,000 Kcs. He had been arrested on a trumped-up political charge and would be in debt for many years, having to find over $720 from a wage of possibly less than $24 per week.

Almost all the prisoners I talked to were disillusioned with communism. I learned that after 1968 there was a big purge of the party in Czechoslovakia, and as a result it is not easy to become a member. Those who do qualify are in a privileged class. The Communists have abolished the three-class system and replaced it with a two-class system which is manifested in many ways. One of these concerns currency. The normal unit of currency in Czechoslovakia is the crown. This is the everyday basis of trade. Ordinary workers are paid in crowns, shops accept them, and tourists receive them in exchange for Western currency. What is not generally known to visitors is that there is a second currency unit in circulation called the Tusex crown, which is worth two and one-half Kcs. With ordinary currency it is possible to buy only goods made in Warsaw Pact countries, whereas with Tusex crowns one can purchase from special shops goods not otherwise obtainable, such as instant coffee, brand-name electrical goods, televisions, tape recorders, Western cars, and clothes. The Tusex can be obtained only by certain party members or by those who have managed to obtain Western currency and exchange it for Tusex at a bank. When in a conversation with the consul, I once let slip my knowledge of their system, the interpreter who was monitoring our conversation turned to me sharply. "How do you know about this?" she demanded, and seemed surprised to hear I had learned it from my cellmates.

Occasionally pressure is put on certain persons to make them join the party. A prisoner told me that his sister, a chemistry graduate doing important research in a pharmaceutical factory, had been offered an increase in salary from 1,500 Kcs a month (approximately $115) to double this figure if she would become a member. Despite this very attractive offer, she had resisted, as morally she could not fulfill the obligations of party membership. I asked the man if he himself were a member. His withering look was answer enough.

"Not even for money?" I asked.

This produced the response I was angling for, as he outlined what membership in the party would involve. He would be allocated to a cell either in his neighborhood or in his place of work, he said, and regularly each month the cell would be given some particular mission. It could be to spy on a workmate and report any subversive activities. Perhaps it would be a call to intimidate some politically suspect individual. Sometimes it would be outright physical persecution of an "offensive" person. As he went on with the list, I saw how impossible it would be for anyone with any moral fiber, let alone a Christian, to become a party member.

When for a short while I was in a cell with some workers imprisoned for theft, I asked them why they risked high penalties for an apparently small gain. I learned that stealing was widespread. They claimed it was impossible to live on the standard rate of pay, so in order to provide simple luxuries, a man is forced to steal. Further up the social scale the same thing applies, but on a more sophisticated level. One man told me that he drove a truck for the state. At the end of his daily eight-hour stint he would go home, disconnect the speedometer cable, then set out to work for himself. He bought state-owned diesel fuel illegally from a friend, and spare parts from someone else who had appropriated them from the state. From his illicit profits my friend had made a good living, with a better-than-average apartment, a car, good clothes for his wife and children, and new furniture. And, of course, all the others in his supply line made their extra profits in the bargain . . . a very good system. Still higher up the scale it became a matter of bribes to lawyers, or gifts to party officials, because even some of the party members are in on the racket.

Whoever I spoke to had a similar story to tell. Even some of the prison staff admitted that there is something wrong with a system which invited such malpractice and can only maintain law and order by force.

On the other hand, I found that almost all the prisoners, especially the would-be escapers, had an exaggerated idea of life in the West. Disillusioned with communism, they judged capitalism by what they could glean from the occasional Western film, television programs received from West Germany or Austria, or the prosperous-seeming tourists who flew into their country, put up at good hotels, and spent lavishly on souvenirs. It did not occur to them that most of these were ordinary working people who had saved for perhaps a couple of years for a holiday abroad. They did not seem to realize that, while in the West luxuries are obtainable, they have to be worked for, and that crossing the border is not a passport to instant success.

Among the many genuinely innocent men, whose only "crime" was a desire to escape from an intolerable system, there were some whose motives were less creditable. I noticed for instance that a high proportion admitted to wanting to avoid family responsibilities such as the payment of maintenance, and others frankly hoped to get rich quick. Others were obvious criminal types, though in our wing of the prison we did not encounter many of these.

All were greatly amused by my own "offense," and tickled by what they considered its originality. Without exception they applauded what I had done and did their best to encourage me to continue the work after I was released. They would spend hours thinking up alternative means of getting Bibles into their country.

10

THE RIGGED TRIAL

The days passed slowly after the visit from Ken and the consul. Up till then, I had been praying desperately that I would be released without trial, either as a result of worldwide publicity, or of the direct intervention of the British government. Not that I was afraid of a trial, but rather I was fully aware that under their system everyone who was held in the prison had to be sentenced to at least long enough to cover the period spent in the *vazba*, or detention wing. Also, given the publicity there had been over my case, if I was tried they would have to find me guilty in order to save face.

During this period the possibility was discussed in certain quarters of my being exchanged for a Czech prisoner in Britain, or of my being ransomed. At one time I was led to think that this latter course might have been followed; the Czech government, along with most eastern bloc states, was short of western currency. However, I was eventually told that it was too late, the matter must now go to court.

It was not until after I returned home that I found out certain facts. A Czech prisoner was in fact being held in the maximum-security prison at Wakefield only six miles from my home. One of the British national daily newspapers sponsored a suggestion that an exchange should be made, although the Czech was in custody, having been sentenced for espionage. His wife came over to visit him and the newspaper wanted to arrange to photograph my wife with his outside the prison, so that they would have a press scoop in the event of the deal going through. However, Zena would not agree, and the proposal never gained any credence with our government. But it did show that such possibilities were in the air.

On October 11 papers were brought to me in my cell indicating that the trial would take place October 27. At this time they also gave me the accusation against me, signed by the prosecutor. As with all previous documents, this was in Czech. As soon as I was able to see my lawyer I complained bitterly that I could not read it. Dr. Strejce told me that he had already asked the prosecutor to have the document translated, but this reasonable request had been bluntly turned down.

This now presented me with a major problem. I had a rough idea of the general accusation against me and could either go into court in two weeks unprepared, or do something about it. But how? Fortunately, by mistake they had put into my cell a well-educated German who knew five languages, including Czech and English. We managed to smuggle in a Czech–English dictionary and, with a prayer for God's help, we set about the task of translating the nine pages of accusation into reasonable English. It took us three days. We used the dictionary to ascertain the exact meaning of the legal preamble. Here are a few extracts:

From enmity against the social, socialist and state foundation of the Republic he has made sedition with a minimum of two persons against the social, socialist and state foundations of the Republic and against allied or friendly relationships of the Republic towards other states and he has committed the above mentioned acts by printing or other equally effective means. . . .

The activity of the accused had all the signs of the penal act of sedition according to paragraph 8/1 and paragraph 100 section 1.a & c. and section 3.a of the Penal Code. The religious literature attacks and distrusts the social and political situation in CSSR in instigating an attack on the allies of the CSSR with the purpose of evoking in the Czech public an enemy mood against the social and state foundations of the CSSR and against their socialist allies. . . . It is also stated that the accused works with an organization which helps Christians in communist countries and that he used many possibilities of transporting Bibles to communist countries. . . .

There is therefore no doubt about the considerable dangerousness of the accused as touching the foundation of our socialist state.

The actual charges against me were as follows:

Para. 100 sec. 3.a. & c. Sedition against the state. Penalty, 5 years.

Para. 148 sec. 1. Evasion of import-export regulations with respect to Bibles. Penalty, 2 years.

Para. 124 sec. 1 & 2.b. Evading customs and import tax on tape recorders and clothing which was in transit. Penalty, 5 years.

Now for the first time I discovered what they were really saying about me, and could understand the reluctance of the prosecutor to allow me to read it. I dared not tell anyone that I knew, not even my lawyer, whom I still treated with a good deal of suspicion.

I had one other piece of knowledge which stood in my favor. Towards the end of my interrogation I had realized that the true purpose of the long questioning and cross-examination was to draw out from me the desired answers to my accusation. This would then enable the prosecuting counsel to bring witnesses and prepare in advance other evidence to counter all my defense. I court I would be defenseless, for I knew my lawyer would do nothing. I believed that by enabling me to see through their methods, God was telling me not to discuss any defense for any point of the accusation. Let them think I had no answer, then spring the answers on them in court when it would be too late for them to bring up counter-accusations. If only I had been prepared for this earlier, I believe I could have beaten them at their own game.

Those waiting days before my trial were nerve racking, but at least I now had some idea what to expect. The charges were ridiculous. My only crime was that I had carried into the country the Word of God and Gospel tracts and literature. Also, I was trying to help the relatives of those who were in prison for their faith. I loved the Czech people for Christ's sake, and this was the reason I was facing trial. I spent all my available time writing out my prepared defense. My lawyer would be of very little value to me. Everything would depend on what I said and did in the courtroom. I was determined that, however they might sentence me, at least I would tell the truth and let God be my judge.

I spent a lot of time in prayer. I knew God was concerned with my case; I was in prison for my service to Him in the cause of the Gospel. The sacrifice I was being called upon to make was nothing; had not Christ been willing in His obedience to the Father, to give up even His life?

The day before my trial, I was praying quietly in the cell when Hans spoke to me. He was a Catholic whom I had been able to help spiritually and bring into a new relationship with Christ.

"What is it the Bible says?" He was speaking in German. "Ask . . . seek . . . knock . . . "?

Suddenly I could have wept. Here I was, troubled and distressed by my predicament, and here was a person whom I had once had to strengthen and encourage to have faith in God, now reminding me of God's promises. In his stumbling way he had pointed me to the Scripture. I remembered the words: "Ask and you shall receive, seek and you shall find, knock and it shall be opened unto you" (*see* Luke 11:9). What greater promise could I have that would give me faith for my forthcoming ordeal? This incident gave me encouragement and strength through the whole of the next day.

I had already been told that Zena had applied for a permit to come to the trial and that she was expected to be there with one of my brothers, as well as the British consul, Mr. McCallion. I had mixed feelings, the thrill of anticipation of seeing her conflicting with worry over the outcome of the trial.

I was awakened early, at five o'clock, for the same rough breakfast which as usual I did not eat, then had to wait until about 5:45 when I was taken to change into my own clothes. Then we went out through a side door where a small, very old Skoda estate car was waiting; they told me it had covered more than 62,000 miles, and it looked like it. My lawyer sat in front with the driver while I was handcuffed and put in the back next to an armed guard. It seemed they were taking no chances. However, to my relief after about twenty minutes the driver turned his head and said something to my guard who produced a key and removed the handcuffs. Shortly afterwards I saw a possible reason for his action. We were running early. The trial was not due to begin until 8:30, yet by about seven o'clock we were not far from Tachov, the town near the border where the trial was to be held. We had just driven down a road which passed close to some woods when unaccountably the driver stopped the car, and without a word got out and walked around to the back. He was gone for some time, and I wondered what was happening. Then one of the other men turned to me and said, "Now is your chance to escape."

Rapidly I assessed the situation. We were very close to the border, only a few yards from some trees which marked the beginning of a wood. At this hour of the autumn morning it was only just getting light and there was a good deal of mist about which would give me all the cover I needed to make a run for it. I glanced around. All I needed to do was hit the guard hard enough to prevent him reaching his gun which was in its holster. It looked like a very inviting opportunity.

As I was wondering whether to make the attempt I suddenly thought of Zena. She would be on the way to the court now; she must be already in the country. It flashed through my mind that if I escaped, they would hold her responsible in some way and probably imprison her on some pretext of assisting me to escape. The thought horrified me. My muscles, already tensed for the spring, relaxed. Better for me to stay in prison than to allow Zena to suffer. I remained sitting in the car. It seemed an eternity before the driver came back and we continued our journey. Only later did I recognize God's providential deliverance. I am convinced now that the whole episode was a trap. They wanted me to escape. No doubt the driver had gone to get a rifle; other soldiers were probably waiting in the woods. It would have been so easy for them to produce my bullet-ridden body and claim, truthfully, that I had been shot while attempting to escape. What a simple and perfect solution to their problem! They would have gotten rid of me in one quick move and the case would have been closed. Even the British newspapers would have mentioned it only in a small column on the inside pages: PRISONER IN CZECHOSLOVAKIA SHOT IN ESCAPE BID.

When we reached our destination I was taken up several flights of stairs to the rooms where the court would sit. There I was put to wait in a small room inside one of the offices. Shortly afterwards my lawyer came through for a few final words with me, and to bring me news that, although my wife would be present at the trial, permission had not been granted for a visit. This meant that she would be allowed to sit at the back of the courtroom but that we would not be able to speak to each other. This news, coming just before the ordeal of the trial itself, upset me more than I would have admitted. This was intolerable! I had not seen Zena for over four months, and our letters had been restricted. I had little idea of what had been happening to her and the children all this time.

Realizing that the time for the trial was drawing near, I asked permission to go to the toilet. The guard motioned me towards the door. As I stepped out into the corridor, there was Zena sitting just in front me, with my brother Ken and Mr. McCallion a few feet away. I rushed up to her and embraced her. Though we did not exchange many words, the thrill of being able to see her again and take her in my arms was wonderful.

After some little time I went back into the room to wait. Now I was told that, after a number of telephone calls between the court and Prague, I would be allowed five minutes to speak to my wife after the trial was over. This was only at the discretion of the president of the court and would have to be in his presence.

Proceedings were about to begin. I was taken across the corridor and into the court. It was a room about twenty feet wide and thirty feet long. In front of me was a long elevated bench where the three judges would sit. To the left, facing inwards at right angles to the judges, was the prosecutor's desk, while facing it on my right was another desk where sat my lawyer, nearest to the bench, and my interpreter, nearest to me. At first I sat in the front row of the chairs which were placed in rows facing the bench while my wife and brother, the consul, and the embassy interpreter sat behind me. The only other person present was the soldier who guarded me, and he sat to one side.

When I went in, the interpreter and my counsel were already seated, and soon afterwards the prosecutor entered. He was a very stout man, middle-aged with thinning hair, impressively dressed in a black gown which he wore wide open to accommodate a sizeable paunch. I had already been warned that he was the worst of all the prosecutors and his stern features and stiff pose only increased my apprehension. Next the three judges appeared and took their places with the girl stenographer. The one on my left was elderly, gray-haired, and rather stern, although I came to look on him as the best one to appeal to during the trial. In the middle sat the president of the court, the oldest of the three. He was the most senior of all the judges at Tachov, apparently the supreme president, the original one having been replaced on this occasion presumably because of the importance of the case. This trial was a major political issue. The youngest judge, to the right, I estimated to be in his forties; he had a boyish face, rather handsome, and he appeared to know it, for his eyes regularly strayed to the direction of the attractive young stenographer. This man I immediately classed as my biggest obstacle because he had the appearance of a man whose job is bigger than he is; probably some minor party official who had been rewarded with this job to get him off someone else's back. All three were impressively robed, in black gowns elaborately lined with purple. The whole thing resembled a stage setting; they were here to make an impression, and to prove that this little state of fourteen million inhabitants could do just as she pleased to a citizen of one of the Western powers.

When all were seated, the trial began. First the prosecutor stood up to make a long opening speech. Since it was all in Czech, it was impossible for me to understand what he said. Occasionally my interpreter would translate something for me, but most of the speech passed over my head. However, it was not difficult to tell from the tone of his voice, his gesticulations, and the venom with which he spoke, that I was being branded as an enemy of the state, a danger to society, and that the innocent biblical literature which I had brought into their country would bring about the downfall of communism if allowed to be distributed.

After he sat down I was cross-examined by the president, who had in front of him a copy of my file consisting of more than two hundred pages of evidence, most of which I had not seen. As I launched into the speech which I had prayerfully written down, they allowed me to speak in my own defense, dealing with the items of the accusation which we had so laboriously translated. Two witnesses were also brought, Jan Kvietok, a customs officer and Vaclava Pucelika, a border policeman from the frontier post at Rozvadov. When called forward, each produced a little red book. I had been told by other prisoners to look out for this book, which is evidence of membership in the Communist party. Neither witness was sworn in to give truthful evidence; members of the party are above the law and their word cannot be questioned.

During my lawyer's speech for the defense I noticed that, whereas while I had been speaking the judges had listened carefully, now they leaned back in their seats obviously disinterested, as if they had heard it all before. Dr. Strejce was brief and unconvincing. Then the prosecutor summed up his accusations, his eyes flaming and his arms waving as, according to my interpreter, he denounced me as guilty and asked for the maximum sentence of five years. After this my lawyer said nothing, but I was allowed to make a final speech in my defense. Halfway through the president interrupted to ask me to make it as short as possible; they were not really interested. Everything I said had to be translated into Czech, but they did not translate everything back to me, so that I was ignorant of what was being said about me. How could I defend myself under such conditions? I felt completely frustrated by it all.

There was a lunch recess for about an hour and a half before we were recalled for the final summing up. During the interval both my wife and the consul were led to believe that the longer the recess continued, the more hopeful the situation would be. It was obvious by now that the whole thing was staged, with my wife and the embassy representatives there to give credence to the legality of the proceedings. Yet, as we were to find out later, in all these political cases, the verdict is not decided in court, but is settled two or three weeks beforehand in a committee meeting of the Communist party somewhere in Prague. A West German doctor whom I met later was sent for a second trial accused of taking drugs into Czechoslovakia. He was taken into court, the judge called a recess, and five minutes later called them back in, announced the verdict, and gave the accused the sentence already typed out. This must have been prepared before the court even sat.

During the waiting period I was comforted by the realization that many hundreds of Christians were meeting at that very time to pray for me; the news of the date of my trial had been widely circulated. I could do nothing but put my faith in God, knowing that He was fighting my case for me. The realization that Zena was in the room with me, and that she knew exactly what I had been doing and was fully in sympathy with it gave me added strength.

I listened to the president's summing up without understanding a single word. Nothing was translated. I was powerless, a pawn in a dangerous political game. My eyes strayed across to the left where the prosecutor sat. There was no mercy in his look. I saw the interpreter making some notes on his pad; leaning forward I saw the number two. So there it was! It could not be two months, it must be two years. My heart sank. Even worse than I had feared!

As the judge sat down, the interpreter began to outline the verdict:

Paragraph 124. Evasion of tax on the tape recorders and clothing I had left openly on the back seat of the bus for declaration that they were in transit. Not guilty; the customs officer had confirmed my evidence that there had not been time or opportunity for them to be declared. However, in the national interest these items were to be confiscated.

Paragraph 148. Failure to make a declaration for import-export of goods in respect to the Bibles and other literature. Minor offense, therefore not to be regarded for punishment.

Paragraph 100. Sedition. " . . . the accused is guilty of enmity against the socialist, social and state foundations of our Republic . . . the offensive literature is capable of evoking enmity against the socialist system of our Republic. . . . He collaborates with an organisation which helps Christians in communist countries . . . and transports Bibles into communist countries. . . . All these printed materials were of offensive and anti-socialist character with religious colouring.

"The penalty is fixed at half the maximum of five years because the offensive literature was confiscated at the border, therefore only an attempt was made but the act was not completed. Also because of the personal circumstances of the accused the sentence is two years. In measuring the penalty the considerable social danger of the action of the accused was taken in account."

I was numb with shock, overcome by a feeling of utter loneliness and despair. My first thought was of my wife and children. Already I had been away from them for over four months. Now I must spend another twenty in that stinking prison. Slowly, without daring to look around me, I walked from the courtroom to wait outside, hoping for a few minutes with Zena. But what could I say to her now?

Eventually I was allowed into the room where the interview was to take place. Zena was there with Ken, the consul, the interpreter, and the court president. Fortunately we were allowed longer than the stipulated five minutes. So many questions. Ken had a whole list of things to ask me . . . about the business . . . the home . . . should they sell my car? So much. Zena was holding my hand tightly, her grasp conveying all the warmth of her love and affection. She would stand by me no matter what the cost, she said, but it would be as hard for her as for me. She would have all the responsibility of the family alone. Who knew when we would meet again?

The others left the room as I embraced her in a last affectionate farewell. Now was my chance. I had come prepared for the worst, so as the guard discreetly turned away I slipped into her pocket a specially prepared secret note in which I had outlined all the action they should take to try to obtain my release. All the information I had been able to glean from inside the prison was packed into that little note. They must now tell the full story to the world, get as much publicity as possible through the press, television, a big campaign of letters of protest, and so much more. The Communists had now done their worst, it was up to my family and friends to do their part.

I walked down the steps of the courthouse with my escort, and out into the open air of the small town. Zena followed behind. I called to her to try to get permission for a visit to see me in Pilsen, then climbed into the waiting car. For the last time I breathed the free air, looked at the gloomy gray of the buildings. Here for a moment was a brief glimpse of freedom, not as we know it in the West, but simply the freedom of air not tainted by the foul stench of prison. A last glimpse of Zena standing there in the fading light with tears in her eyes. A last wave, and she was gone; but the memory of the girl I loved standing there trying not to cry, to be as brave as she could, was the memory that would have to carry me through the bleak weeks and months ahead.

11

THE HOPELESS APPEAL

My mind was in a turmoil as we drove back to Pilsen. It would take time to get over the shock of the verdict, for I had prayed so hard that I would be acquitted. How was it possible that I had been cleared of all charges of smuggling, yet found guilty of sedition? Then, when I had asked my lawyer before the trial what the maximum sentence was likely to be, he had inferred that if we failed altogether, the most I could expect would be twelve to eighteen months. But two years!

Zena was in my thoughts all this time. How was she taking it? What would she do? Before I had left the courtroom I had pleaded with the president as well as Dr. Strejce to be allowed a visit from her at Bory prison. They had said that they would try to get permission, but that she must wait a few days as it would take time to obtain. Also, it would be necessary for either the president of the court or one of his staff to be present at the visit. Back in my dreary cell, I could not eat or sleep. Lying on the hard iron bedstead, my thoughts were all of Zena and the three girls, Sharon and Carol, twins sixteen years old, and the youngest, little Mandy, who would have her fourth birthday in just ten days' time. She had so much wanted a bike and I promised her one last summer, for her birthday. "She will be nearly six when I get home," I thought. "Sharon and Carol will be eighteen." Then I fell to wondering how Zena would manage without me. What were her reactions now that the trial was over? She had always been a little too dependent on me, and now everything would fall on her shoulders.

I remembered the day I first met Zena, the girl who became my wife. It was 1953, our Queen's coronation year. In January she had won a local beauty contest in the nearby town of Knaresborough where she lived with her parents. As Miss Knaresborough she had many opportunities to enjoy herself and was the envy of the other girls in the neighborhood as well as the main attraction to the local boys who sought her favor. In May of that year we had a crusade in Harrogate, at the church where I was a young pastor. Zena came, and found Christ there. Her life was radically changed. From then on she found herself more and more involved in the activities of the church, which gave her less and less time for the pursuit of pleasure. At the time I lived in lodgings very near her, so as she often played the piano for me at the church, it seemed quite natural for me to give her a lift home in my car. I soon began to fall for this golden-haired beauty who so willingly assisted me in the church and even began to give up her official duties to help me.

A vivid memory of our courtship days was of the carnival evening that September. As in other years, there had been a procession earlier in the day in which Zena had taken part, and now the day's festivities were to be crowned by the water carnival, on the river Nidd which flows picturesquely and romantically through the small town of Knaresborough. The setting was especially lovely on that still warm evening of late summer. Afterwards there was to be a supper attended by all the civic dignitaries at which Zena needed to be present. Her father had arranged to pick her up from the waterside to bring her home, but it did not take me long to persuade him that it would be far too late for him to be out, well past his bedtime, which was a family joke. I knew there were plenty of other young men who would be lining up for the privilege.

I was busy with church duties for the first part of the evening, but as soon as I could I drove the three miles from Harrogate to Knaresborough, parked my car in a convenient position and went to watch the remainder of the evening's program. It was most spectacular, including a procession of decorated floats and a mock sea battle between fleets of ships lined up on the water. It was a lovely evening, I was to take home the Queen of the Carnival, what more could a young man want? Shortly before the end, I slipped away to fetch my car, ready for the moment when I could proudly drive up in front of the others to collect my prize.

Trouble! One of my tires was as flat as a pancake. And my only spare had itself burst a couple of days earlier, and as a poor parson I had not been able to afford a replacement. What could I do? I found myself praying, "Please God, help me." There was only one thing to be done. I removed the wheel and rolled it down the road to an all-night garage. This took some time and the only man on duty was only there to pump gasoline and would not mend a puncture. Impatiently I looked around inside the garage and found there was another car identical to mine, with its wheels off. After some persuasion the man on duty let me borrow one of the wheels. Was it my insistence, was he half-asleep, or was it another of those miracles with which God sometimes helps those who cannot help themselves? I pushed the wheel all the way up the hill to where my car had been abandoned. A few minutes and it was in place. A quick dash to the appointed place, a glance at my watch, a sigh of relief. I had made it, and in time! A few moments later, Zena came out and we drove off together.

Nobody except the garage man would know what near tragedy had marred my triumph.

Or so I thought. Next evening, when I called again at the home, the family were laughing over someone Zena's sister had seen the previous evening — an unfortunate young man rolling a wheel up the hill to a broken-down car stranded at the roadside. My secret was out . . . which made Zena laugh louder than ever. But mine was the last laugh and the longest, for eleven months later we announced our engagement and eight months later still we married in the church in Harrogate where we had first met. It was a lovely April day and the church was so crowded that many stood in the street outside while my father performed the simple ceremony.

For us, this was just the beginning of a shared work, at first in the church, then in the growing travel business, finally in the work of the ministry to the suffering thousands behind the Iron Curtain. We had shared everything, joy as well as suffering. Now, as I thought so much of the girl I had left behind, I realized that this was to be her biggest heartache.

In 1961, when I had set off on the trip to Jerusalem, to me it had been excitement and adventure. Only when I returned home did I find out from my closest friend how Zena had cried her eyes out when I had driven off. When pressure built up to repeat the trip, she did not stand in my way. Again, as the business grew over the years, she gave in. Now she was alone. I could stand what they were doing to me; men who serve God must be willing to suffer, even to die for their faith. Even one of the prison police interpreters had said quietly to me one day, "How I admire your faith; even to us you are a hero." But Zena, could she stand up to all that would be involved in the next days and months? So I prayed, "Please, God, let Zena be given permission to talk to me." If only I could have the opportunity to strengthen her, to reassure her. But God said no. Still, throughout the time I spent in prison, it was the certainty of Zena's love and her understanding that did most to strengthen me. Many people must have seen the television program soon after my trial, when one of my brothers, asked whether he agreed with what I was doing, avoided answering the question rather than offend the Czechs. Zena was then asked the same question, and without hesitation and fearing no one she replied that she fully agreed with it and was proud of what I had done.

For the first five or six days after my trial I could not eat and it was to be a long time, nearly two weeks, before I could sleep properly again. Desperately I waited for Zena to come. Surely permission must come through for a visit. Each day that dawned brought new hope, each day that ended was the death of that hope. I could only wait and pray. At the end of a week hope had almost gone, but still I clung on. It finally died altogether on November 7, eleven days after the trial, and Mandy's fourth birthday. That was a particularly bad day. My thoughts were so much on both Mandy and Zena that it would have taken very little to make me explode. Till now I had taken things as calmly as possible; I had expected either release or a minimum sentence. Now the tension built up within me; even now I can see myself pacing up and down the tiny exercise yard, controlling myself with difficulty. I could not understand the attitude of the British government. Was it merely a "paper tiger" as other nations claimed? I was convinced then, and remain so today, that there would be much more respect for Britian in the international sphere if the Foreign Office had more backbone instead of wishbone.

November 10 was an important day. The prosecutor had two weeks from the time of the trial in which he could appeal against my sentence. I had the same time. As Dr.

Strejce informed me, this posed a tricky situation. If the prosecutor appealed, then the appeal court had two alternatives, either to keep the sentence or increase it. If I appealed, the sentence would either remain the same or be reduced. This meant that whoever made the appeal had an immediate advantage. If both of us did so, the advantage was cancelled out. From his knowledge of the prosecutor, Dr. Strejce advised me not to appeal until the last day. If I did so earlier, the prosecutor would inevitably appeal also. If I did not appeal, then found that he had, I should be in difficulty. So I put in my appeal on the last day, just praying that the prosecutor would not do the same. Dr. Strejce came to see me again on November 15 and told me the verdict. Though mine was the only appeal, he warned me not to expect any reduction; he thought that the sentence would stand. Now I must wait another four or five weeks for the appeal to be heard.

I was determined to go through with the appeal, although I was told that I could now withdraw it. My reasons were, first to contest a ridiculous verdict and fight for my freedom; second to make every possible protest to the Czech authorities to show them that I would not take this sentence lying down. How could I later protest against the sentence unless I used every legal means at my disposal to fight it? Third, I wanted the Czech government to publicly substantiate their reasons for branding Christian literature as seditious when their constitution supposedly guaranteed religious freedom. It was, after all, for political sedition that I had been sentenced, and explicitly not for smuggling.

Most of the interim period was devoted to going over both the accusation and the sentence, which I again had to translate for myself as it was inevitably handed to me in Czech. I wrote out my defense point by point, and since

I was able to smuggle out my notes, I can quote them in detail.

The appeal was fixed for Wednesday, December 13, in the supreme court at Pilsen, near the prison. My family could not come this time, but the consul was again present in person. I was, and still am, very grateful to him for the support he gave me in those difficult days.

I based my defense mainly on the nature of the literature concerned, which was listed as 2,862 pieces of religious material (that is, Bibles, hymnbooks, and New Testaments) plus 900 copies of a religious tract entitled *Proč ?* — *"Why?"* My major points were:

1. *PROČ?*

(*a*) I had no knowledge of the existence of this leaflet.

(*b*) I did not load the literature into the compartment. This statement confirmed by the driver and the other passengers on the bus.

(*c*) It was impossible in any case to know the contents of the leaflet as it was in Czech. I do not understand one word of the language. (It was partly in order to emphasize this point in my defense that I had refused to learn the language while in prison.)

(*d*) The wording of the sentence says, "that in a hidden manner[the leaflet]attacks the state." If it was hidden, how should I know that it attacked the state, even if I understood what the tract said?

(*e*) I do not know the contents of the tract. Will the court please tell me one thing that is seditious about it?

(*f*) During my interrogation I was told by the interrogating police that all that is contained in the tract is found in the Bible. Therefore if the tract is seditious, then the Bible is also seditious.

(*g*) There is no actual evidence to prove that I knew

116

the contents, only an assumption by the SVD and the court.

2. THE BIBLE

(*a*) Under the reasons given by the court at Tachov for finding me guilty it is clearly stated: "All these printed materials were of an offensive and anti-socialist character." That means the Bible is seditious.

(*b*) The sentence of the court many times refers to the "offensive printed materials and leaflets." Therefore the printed materials (Bibles) are clearly marked as being seditious in addition to the tracts (leaflets).

(*c*) All the proofs offered by the court at Tachov, as quoted in the sentence, refer specifically only to Bibles. Not one refers to the tract. Therefore the whole prosecution case is made out only on the premise that I brought Bibles into the country, yet I am accused of sedition, not smuggling.

(*d*) The Bible cannot be seditious according to Czech law. The constitution clearly states that religious freedom is guaranteed. To have the Bible or religious material cannot be a crime.

There were many other points which I raised, but these are enough to show the weakness of the charges. In reply the court could not justify any single point of the sentence. They refused to read out the tract, they refused to tell me one point on which it was seditious. Also, which is the most serious aspect of the trial, they refused to acknowledge the statement in their own constitution guaranteeing religious freedom. There is no religious freedom in Czechoslovakia and my trial and subsequent sentence are irrefutable evidence of this.

Looking at the translation of the verdict of the appeal

court, given me at my request by the British embassy in Prague, I find the only thing they can say against the tract *Proč?* is that "by quotations from the Bible it attacks the socialist state." They then go on with a long statement of the ideological differences between Christianity and communism.

Throughout my interrogation, imprisonment, and trial, one point was constantly made clear to me by the SVD as well as the prison officers and the court. I was only there because I had brought into the country "that filthy and offensive book," the Bible. That is how they really think of it, in spite of their claims, for foreign consumption, that they print the Bible and allow it to be distributed.

After all the evidence had been heard, the prosecutor asked for one of three courses to be taken. The first was that my sentence should be increased; this was impossible. The second, that it should stay as it was. The third, which caused me some anxiety, was that the verdict of the first court should be set aside and the case referred back for retrial. This was the last thing I wanted. It would take another six weeks for a new trial, at which anything could happen, including a stiffer sentence, and an appeal, if one were necessary, could add another six weeks — a total of three more months in the detention wing. So it was with something like relief that I heard the president of the court pronounce the verdict, that the sentence would remain unchanged, though the charge was modified.

The only positive outcome of the appeal was that the court clearly stated that several tape recorders, electric razors, and items of clothing should be returned to me. These had been held by the authorities since my arrest owing to the fact that I had originally been charged with evading customs duty on them. The first court had acquitted me of this charge, but despite this had found a paragraph under which it could confiscate them "in the national interest." Now the appeal court declared such action illegal and ruled that the goods should be returned to me. The value placed on them by the Czechoslovak authorities was about 20,000 Kcs or $1,700. So far, they have not been returned to me, nor have I received any compensation for them.

One other thing the court made clear. Tremendous pressure had been brought to bear following my sentence on October 27. My wife and brother had returned home to find that the trial had had nationwide coverage by press and television. This in turn resulted in a buildup of worldwide public opinion, questioning why a man should be arrested and sentenced for taking Bibles into a country. The Czechs clearly did not like the inference that they oppressed Christians. As a direct result of this, and of my insistence in court that I could not be sentenced on a charge of sedition with regard to the Bibles, the appeal court changed the original verdict to state that:

By appeal of the accused, the sentence passed by the District Court at Tachov on the 27/10/72, is completely annulled and a new sentence has been passed on the accused, according to paragraph 259 sec. 3 of the criminal law.

The accused is not being punished and has not been sentenced for bringing Bibles, the New Testament, religious songs and other religious literature into the country, but because he brought in for distribution the leaflet *Proč?* that is, literature which by quotations from the Bible attacks the principles of a socialist state and was aimed at turning the citizens of that socialist state against the political and cultural life of the state and against the building of socialism.

No further legal appeal can be made against this sentence.

119

So, I was not being sentenced for bringing in Bibles, but quotations from the Bible which "attacked the principles of a socialist state." Add to this the fact that I made three separate requests to be allowed to have my own Bible in the cell and on each occasion was refused on the grounds that it was an offensive book and should be banned. How can the Czech government claim that there is freedom of religion? The court knew that I was a Christian minister, that I had no political leanings, that all the literature was of a purely religious character. Two responsible persons, one a lawyer, the other a police interpreter, had both stated categorically that the leaflet was not seditious and would normally be allowed. These were Czech citizens. I could only draw one inference. The leaflet *Proč?* was being used as an excuse; even without it I would still have been held, probably on a charge of "ideological subversion."

The reason for this was clear. I was originally charged with bringing into Czechoslovakia the Bible which was "seditious."Yet how could it be, if they claimed to have religious freedom and allow Bibles to be printed there for propaganda purposes? Embarrassed that their true feeling came out in an official record, they tried to switch attention from the Bibles. But it was clear from the beginning: **it was their hatred of the Bible which was at the core of it all.** No amount of maneuvering could change that. It was that "filthy book" which they hated and feared, and wanted to keep from their people.

It was now December 13. I had to wait for the sentence to be delivered to me, then I would be sent from the *vazba* into the prison proper to serve out my sentence. The question was, which prison would it be? I had heard that most foreign prisoners were sent to a special prison in Prague. However, at Tachov I had heard the president of the court say that it would probably be the political wing in Pilsen. That was what I most feared. We had heard over the prison grapevine of the appalling conditions there, the food even more restricted than normal, increased work loads, visiting and letters severely restricted; most sinister of all, the "medical supervision" was, according to the medical staff themselves, designed to eliminate the prisoners. These facts were confirmed by a prisoner in our cell who had spent a short time there. I begged the consul to use the British government's influence to get me sent to Prague, where I would at least be near the embassy. I wondered when I would be transferred. Would I spend Christmas in the *vazba*?

On the nineteenth, the seventh day after the appeal, the cell door was suddenly opened and I was given curt orders to collect my things. This meant moving into an escort cell on the floor above. Here I found four others, all waiting like me for transfer to the prison where the sentence would be served. Now for the first time I was with ordinary criminals. They spoke reasonably good German, and I learned from them a great deal about life under communism. One told me straight that as workers what they wanted was a capitalist state such as we had in Britain. They said they could not live under communism.

Wednesday the twentieth I remember because I was called out of the cell to receive a large-sized packet. It was not a Christmas parcel, but inside was a Christmas card from my daughters. It was the biggest card I had ever seen. I was so thrilled, my eyes filled with tears as I read what they had written inside: "To the most wonderful Dad in the world. We shall not see you but we shall not forget you, you will ever be in our thoughts." I kept that card with me till the day I left prison. Many other prisoners, and even the officers, commented on it.

Later that day we were told to prepare to leave the next morning for a new prison. We cheered up; this was good news, anything must be better than the horrors of Bory.

We were awakened at five o'clock. There were five of us, but only two early breakfasts. Our hearts sank . . . only two going? We knew that the transfer of prisoners took place only once a week. Those who did not go today would have to stay until next Thursday at the earliest. That meant Christmas in the escort cell, a most unpleasant prospect, for these cells were dirty, broken down, and neglected. We asked the officer which of us would be going. He pointed out one of the other men . . . then mentioned my name.

Then came the procedure of transfer, or "escort." Stripped, we were submitted to a personal search, then allowed to put on our own clothes and given any personal belongings. Most of the others had a few personal things in brown paper parcels. One or two had a small travelling bag. I had three suitcases and a very large cardboard box. The reason was that in addition to my own luggage I had part of the clothing that had been destined for the Christians in Rumania. No one else on the bus had acknowledged it, so it had been classed with my personal luggage.

All this had to go with me, the other prisoners kindly helping me to carry it to the escort bus. They were intrigued by the nature of my "crime," and sympathetic towards me.

As the bus drove away in the dark of the wintry morning I saw for the first time what this prison really looked like from the outside, the gray exterior of the walls, the watchful sentries in the towers. Suddenly I could no longer hold back the tears. I wept unashamedly, not for my own suffering, not for all that had passed during six months. No, I wept because for the first time I saw that all these people in this country were living in a gigantic prison camp. They needed freedom, deliverance, salvation. They were as desperate as I was, their need was greater than mine. After another eighteen months I could hope to be expelled from the country; they must live forever condemned to an existence not of their own choosing. I realized that communism has become not an ideology but a prison, not a system where all men are free and equal but one where men's lives are governed by fear and barbed wire. I wept because, humanly speaking, there is no hope for them; they must live and die under this yoke of oppression. These were the people Christ came to free. Did He not come to a nation in bondage under the oppression of the Romans? Czechoslovakia cries out for freedom; the word the people write on the walls by night in white paint is *Proč?* — Why? Their need for Christ was even greater than mine.

It was at midday on December 21 that the bus pulled into the gates of Pancrac prison right in the center of Prague. I had been exactly six months to the day in that other prison. How long would I spend here? I was taken to reception, stripped again, given a different uniform. This was ex-army stuff, a full uniform, overcoat, boots, coarse underwear, overalls for work, enough to last me for a long sentence. The thought depressed me. Then along the corridors, through the iron gates, the bars, the lock, the guard. Now I was with just one other man, a German. A door opened, I was thrust inside. An English voice spoke my name: "You must be David Hathaway, we have been expecting you."

I was in a prison within a prison. This was the "foreign department." Here only Western foreigners were sent. These men were German, French, Austrian, Arab, and many other nationalities. The man who had greeted me was an English-speaking German. Soon I was to see others whom I recognized. There was Alex, who had been with me way back last June in cell fifty-four in Bory; he had six years. Then there was Wolfgang, whom I had met occasionally in the exercise yard; he had fourteen months. The tall, blond German who had first greeted me was called Christian; he had a six-year sentence. It seemed that my name and reputation had preceded me. They knew all about my "crime." I was soon to find that many of them were no more guilty of any crime than I was; they, too, were the victims of political warfare, pawns in a gigantic game which enables masterminds to control the destiny of the innocent.

In a few days it was Christmas. This was the most traumatic experience of all.

On Christmas Eve the four of us in my cell, Christian, Helmuth, George, and I, with Wolfgang from the next cell, sat at our rough table. The others had pooled what food they had with the extras that had come in Christmas parcels. I had nothing, no parcels had arrived for me to give a little cheer to the gloom in the cell. Of the two which my wife had sent, one arrived in February, the other just didn't arrive. For most of us, especially those with wives and children, this was a time which we could gladly forget. Several men had been attending the doctor for psychiatric treatment and had received supplies of tranquilizers. These they carefully hoarded so that now in their misery they could take as many pills as possible, desiring more than anything to blot out all memories of home, of wives, of children, of past Christmases, even of happiness itself. They, like me, only wanted to forget . . . their greatest wish, oblivion.

Those who were fortunate enough to have this means of escape lay down and spent Christmas as far from reality as possible. For the rest of us it meant living with our thoughts and memories. There was nothing to take our minds off home. How can I describe what followed? Waking on Christmas morning, dreading lest I should give way and the others should see my tears. What would Mandy be doing? I loved her so much. I could imagine her eyes opening in wonder; what questions would she be asking? "Where is my Daddy? Why hasn't he come home yet?" The others were old enough to understand, to comfort their mother. Mandy was too young to know, just questions with no answer. It was a terrible time. I repeated over and over again, "Why me? Why me?" Yet through all this I remembered that God had so loved the world that He sent His Son, at Christmas, knowing full well that it meant sorrow, suffering, death. He was willing, and so must I be. This Christmas I'm giving more to God than I ever have before . . . this is the path of service. Wasn't Paul in prison, Silas, and Peter as well? I'm not alone. . . . But sometimes, oh, God! it is more than we can bear. Why does God let us suffer? Yet suffering is the only way that some of us can really get close to God.

After that we tried to forget Christmas and get on with the reality of prison existence. Soon it was New Year. Where would I be next Christmas? If only this were just a dream and I would soon awake from the nightmare of it all!

12

LIFE IN PANCRAC PRISON

Pancrac was classed as a "group two" prison according to the Czech system. After the rigors of Bory, where we had all been put together, Czech nationals as well as Westerners, to face the torments of interrogation, the prisoners were separated into various categories according to the severity of their sentence, and sent to other prisons or labor camps to serve out their time. Group-three prisoners, in the most severe category, are sent to forced labor; some go on to the uranium mines. We heard some terrible stories of what can happen to them as a result of exposure to radiation. Those who survive to the end of their sentence are likely to be crippled for life.

Group-two prisoners are also subjected to long, hard labor, but in conditions less arduous than those of the camps and the mines. Officially, with most of the other foreigners, I was classed as group one. However, in order to prevent us from infecting the Czech prisoners with our bourgeois Western ideology, we were locked away in a small section of Pancrac isolated from the other prisoners, in effect a maximum-security section. Whereas the other 2,500 prisoners could mix freely during both work and recreation, we were never allowed out of our tiny section, except for the occasional official visit or for medical attention. All our food, and even our work, was brought to us in the *Ausland Abteilung* as it was called, using the German designation.

There were about two dozen of us at any one time; the number varied slightly as men were admitted or released. Our accommodation consisted of six cells in a row, with a narrow corridor running the length of the section. At the far end, nearest to the door which cut us off from the main prison, was another short stretch of corridor, about four yards in length, then an iron grille, and next to it a washroom with a long metal trough and water taps as well as a small shower cubicle. The cells, each opening off the right of the corridor, were uniform in size, six feet wide by twelve feet long. Each contained four metal bed frames arranged two by two, in bunk fashion, leaving barely enough room for a small iron or wood table and four chairs. In addition there was a wooden cupboard which held our aluminum army dishes for meals, any cutlery we could scrounge in addition to the regulation spoon, and the remains of such food parcels as we were allowed to supplement our bare and unpalatable diet.

At the end of the row of cells was a slightly wider room, officially called the recreation room, where the more fortunate of us, myself included, fulfilled our daily work norms. At least we had a window. The others had to work in the corridor, on narrow benches fastened to the wall. Because we were not allowed out, we could not be employed on heavy manual labor like other group-two prisoners, but on two days a week we worked with lead, cutting and shaping metal weights, while the rest of the time was spent making paper flags, cardboard boxes, or thick paper bags.

Our day officially began at 5:30. Invariably, though, I was awakened at about 4:45 by the sound of the Czech prisoners being drilled, military fashion, outside the small cell window. These unfortunates were awakened soon after four o'clock and even in midwinter, in conditions of

127

frost and snow, they had to face this early muster in the exercise yard. The sound of several hundred marching feet and the shouted commands of "*Ras, Dva*" echoing from the encircling walls was enough to wake the dead, let alone weary prisoners with aching limbs and empty stomachs. This rude awakening each morning was a dramatic and brutal reminder of the horror of our situation and our total separation from the outside world of home and family. I never got used to it. It caused me to face each new day with a feeling of dread that is impossible to describe in retrospect. As with so much in that Communist prison, it was the atmosphere as much as anything that colored our daily lives and filled us with apprehension.

Often the guards would come into our section, especially in the evenings, and walk around the cells examining with envious eyes the various items of food which came in our parcels. They explained that it was impossible for them to obtain such things as Nescafé and tinned meat. Until recently, I understood, Czechoslovakia had not manufactured margarine because the government had put a priority on producing arms and ammunition to the detriment of consumer goods.

One of the guards, known to us as Peter, used to take pleasure in taunting us, "You will not easily get out of here. I will be in the West before you are," the inference being that he would escape if he could to the better life he was convinced lay beyond the barbed wire and minefields of the borders.

Each evening we had roll call at 6:30, when we all had to line up in the corridor to be counted by one of the duty officers. They always came in pairs, and more than once the officer in charge was so drunk that he could not stand up but would lean on a chair or workbench while his companion checked us, and then they staggered out together.

128

Although Pancrac was a male prison, the foreign department was an exception. Any women from the West were held in a special section to which the only access was through our quarters. Double doors separated their quarters from ours and we were never allowed to mix. The only times these doors were opened were when the officers brought in work or food. For most of the time I was in Pancrac, only one woman lived in this part; another, who was ill, was confined to the hospital until she was eventually expelled and repatriated. Our neighbor was about fifty years old and apparently of French nationality. She existed under appalling conditions, virtually in solitary confinement. From what I gathered from other prisoners, she was ill for much of the time, and she was so cut off that during the night she had no means of calling for assistance; even in the daytime we could only communicate with her by banging on the connecting door, so that she had to wait until an officer came in order to indicate her needs.

For a short while there was a second woman with her, younger, probably in her thirties. This was the period when frequently two of the officers would pass through our section late at night, usually carrying bottles of drink. They would stay for some time in the women's quarters, then return through our section to get out. We were supposed to be in our cells at the time, but it was obvious to us, listening as well as seeing, what was going on. We knew how long the visits were, and how frequent. The conditions in which the women in Pancrac are kept ought to be investigated by the Red Cross.

Among the men in my section there was an Austrian name Sladek. We all knew that he was an informer, and he was hated by most of the others. For some time before my arrival he had been the officially appointed "brigadier" and had ruled the whole department by fear, constantly reporting prisoners so that they ended up in the punishment cells for nothing at all. He openly declared that he would turn the whole department into a concentration camp with its attendant atrocities. Eventually, he took things too far and found himself sent to the punishment cells in his turn. He was evil, immoral, sadistic in the extreme, and he became an object of derision and hatred even to the guards. Although by the time I arrived he had been replaced as brigadier, his influence was still felt and he carried out his activities in a more subtle way by informing on us and making regular reports to the officers in charge. I have subsequently learned that after I left, the other prisoners searched his cell and found evidence of incriminating reports on several of his comrades. They took him into the workroom late one night and severely beat him up, smashing a heavy wooden chair in the process.

One of the more entertaining characters was Ahmed, an Arab from Bagdhad, who went around telling his story to anyone who would listen. Since he spoke English quite well, we often used to talk together. As a captain in the Iraqi army, he had become involved in a political intrigue and had incurred the death penalty. He did the only possible thing. He fled the country and went to live in Damascus where he took up drug smuggling, and was eventually arrested at Prague airport for carrying narcotics.

Ahmed learned from his lawyer that he could expect a two-year sentence, followed by repatriation — which in his case meant certain and ignominious death. He saw no point in serving two years in a Communist jail only to be hanged at the end of it. Better to get it over with straight away. He did his best at his trial to disrupt the court, swearing at the judge and making rude comments about the interpreter, but to his disappointment he still only got six years. He wrote to the president of the republic begging for the death penalty, without result. For weeks he went about in a state of gloom, bemoaning his fate. "Six years they want to keep me here. Why will they not let me die now?" Then came a sudden change in the political situation in Iraq, and Ahmed's party was back in favor. His despair was comic as he realized that, had he been given only two years, he might soon have been a free man. He had done eighteen months by the time I left.

Of course, many of the prisoners were criminals, among them other drug smugglers, thieves, and con men. But many were innocent, or had committed only trivial offenses. Quite a number were in for trying to help others escape from the country; their sentences ranged from six months for helping a fiancée to six years when a group of people was involved. Several western tourists, particularly from Germany, were in for motoring offenses. Those who had been involved in accidents, particularly when drink was involved, received sentences of up to two and a half years. Two men had five and six months respectively for buying antique coins in Czechoslovakia with West German deutschmarks. Their offense was not in buying the coins but in changing the money illegally other than in a bank. Another had twelve months for buying an East German camera legally but with money changed on the black market.

Perhaps the most unfortunate case was that of a tourist who had his expensive fur coat stolen in a restaurant. He complained to the manager, who called the police and they put him in a cell. When he protested that the cell was filthy and not fit for pigs to live in, he was accused of calling Communists filthy pigs and sentenced to sixteen months. Another man had gone to the help of his brother, who had become involved in a minor traffic offense. In the course of the interview he himself was searched and documents were found indicating that he had committed a

131

petty breach of currency regulations. He got ten months. The sad thing was that his brother was released the next morning.

Three or four of the prisoners from our department were taken away after serving their first sentences and given a further trial and sentence on other charges. This made us all aware that we could by no means be sure of eventual release, especially as we knew that we had at least one informer in our midst.

Though we were not allowed to mix with the Czech prisoners, the prison grapevine provided as always an effective means of contact. There was one particular prisoner who had to visit our section regularly; I cannot identify him, since he has a long sentence and will still be inside as you read this. He became my contact with the rest of the prison, and as he spoke good English we could talk easily without being overheard by the guards. It was through him that I was able to contact Czech Christian prisoners and exchange information. In this way I learned of the persecution of believers and of pastors who were in Pancrac for their faith in Christ. When I left in 1973, these men were still inside. One pastor was sentenced to twelve months' hard labor simply for inviting people to attend a Gospel service.

Group-two prisoners like those in Pancrac were not treated with maximum severity but they were made to work long hours, beaten, and abused; often they were treated worse than animals. All Communists are used to working to a norm, which is a given amount of work which they must complete in a day or a week. But in Pancrac the norms were raised so high that the prisoners had to suffer in order to reach the target and failure to do so meant further punishment, usually in the punishment cells. This was not the only kind of suffering they had to endure. Most of the married prisoners in our department had problems with their wives. Several were being sued for divorce. The interrogating police used mental and psychological methods which could result in the breakdown of marriages and family relationships; this was designed both to make the prisoners crack and to increase the severity of their punishment.

I used to talk a great deal with Christian and Wolfgang, both to improve my German and to help them with some of the finer points of English. Naturally we spent a lot of time discussing conditions in the prison. Wolfgang, who had completed his final exams in the university to qualify as a doctor, confirmed what most of us thought, that under the prevailing conditions any person who spent a prolonged period in the prison would suffer irreversible mental and psychological changes. We felt that the limit for normal persons would be about two years, after which time most prisoners would be permanently affected. We were able to see this dramatically in the cases of many who had sentences of four, six, and even eight years. Some whose sentences were completed during my stay went out physical and mental wrecks. Others, still inside, became violently antisocial or mentally unbalanced, or turned into sadists. Contributing factors were the lack of protein, minerals, and vitamins in the diet, poor medical attention, lack of exercise, and the lasting effects of the earlier period of interrogation. Some developed open sores which would not heal, others went gray or lost their hair. I had become covered with a rash on my face and boils all over my body. Then one day I had a heart attack.

It happened on January 14, not long after my removal to Prague. In spite of the severe pain, I was made to walk to the doctor before being taken on a stretcher to the prison hospital for a check and an electrocardiograph. As it was after five o'clock, the only people who could read the EKG had gone off duty so I was sent back to my cell, with no permission to stop work. The next day I had to continue working until I was sent for another EKG. Though it showed some faults, the woman doctor pronounced me fit enough, gave me some tablets, and sent me back to work.

Apart from genuine illness, often men would resort to all sorts of ruses to try to escape from the intolerable burden of work. The prison officers in Pancrac told us that there is a special museum there of objects which prisoners have swallowed. One man had swallowed spoons twelve times, and each time they had operated and removed the spoon, sending him back to work. The thirteenth time they sewed him up, the wound would not heal because of the number of previous scars, and he died.

The prison dentists were no less ruthless than the doctors. I was fortunate, as a foreigner, to get some repair work done, but a Czech with whom I shared a cell in Bory for a time complained of a toothache and promptly had the tooth pulled out without any anaesthetic injection. I was told that this was always so with Czech nationals.

When to all the physical hardships there was added the fact that very few of the prisoners ever had visits from their wives or girl friends, our feeling of total isolation from the real world was complete. During those dark and desperate days, I am convinced, it was only the reality of my contact with God in prayer that kept me sane.

13

THE FIGHT TO BOOST MORALE

It is difficult to describe adequately the strains of prison life. Living in a small cell for a long period with four other men, with little opportunity for exercise, had its own problems. In Bory, the fact that we were all under interrogation, with the attendant mental and psychological tension, had aggravated the situation. Added to this was the fact that during the first three and a half months no one with me spoke any English, so that I could not understand one word of the babel of Czech going on around me, my only contact with my companions being through the few words of German which I knew and the even fewer they did. During my six months in the *vazba* we were kept under constant harassment by the prison officers, the whole process designed to break us down both physically and mentally, so that we would eventually crack and confess our crimes in order to escape the horrifying conditions.

They had said that they would not use physical torture but, reduced to these conditions, it was like living only one step away from hell. This, added to the fact that letters to and from my wife were deliberately delayed for up to three months, was psychological torture.

On many occasions when the strain in the cell became intolerable, fights broke out among the prisoners. Conversation had to be guarded because of the very real fear of informers. Reports would filter through to us of the beatings given to some of the other Czech prisoners in adjoining cells. Sometimes there would be the sight or the sound of a body being carried out.

The officers reviled me for being a Christian. As news of my offense spread among the prison staff, they would open the door as they passed and call out some variation of the same theme: "You are a filthy Christian, you brought these lying books into our country. We will see that you are punished severely. The British government cannot help you, not even your God. Praying will not get you out. You can die in here." Hans would translate their remarks to me, but often he was reluctant to do so, merely saying, "You are fortunate that you do not speak Czech."

The important thing in prison is to find some way to boost morale. Otherwise one soon becomes crushed and defeated. I saw how the other prisoners grew cowed and submissive, brainwashed by the constant pressure. I was determined that this would not happen to me. I would maintain my integrity and my Christian witness.

In Bory, during our brief exercise periods, the others would use the time as an opportunity to smoke and to talk to the men from the neighboring cell who joined us. I do not smoke, and realizing the importance of exercise. I would run or walk briskly around the tiny yard. Gradually, some of the Czechs were persuaded to join me. This caused the officers watching to comment favorably. Also, although open prayer was obviously forbidden, I found ways of praying regularly, thus maintaining contact with God.

I kept up a constant battle with the authorities. This had two purposes. Partly it was to keep up my own morale; also, it was designed to cause them the maximum embarassment, in the hope that they would eventually want to get rid of me.

My first action had been to protest directly to the prison commander about the appalling and primitive conditions. Then I became very concerned at the long time it was taking for my letters to reach Zena and for her replies to come back. Eventually, shortly before my trial, letters stopped coming from home altogether. My only contact with Zena and the girls was broken. I was so furious with the prison authorities, or rather the SVD whose decision I suspected it was, that I wrote in English a strong letter of protest to the Ministry of the Interior in Prague, complaining in the most forceful terms I could muster. This letter I handed in at about nine o'clock one morning, to go either via the censor or through my SVD interrogators. At eleven I was summoned to a room where were present the commandant of the section and the prosecutor (whom I would later meet in the appeal court). Speaking in German the prosecutor handed me six letters, asking me to sign a receipt for them, then told me as politely as possible that he was sorry for the delay and that there were no more.

It was obvious that my letter to the ministry had been checked urgently by one of the censors and reported to the officers responsible, who acted quickly before the letter was sent. I soon found out that even the Communist officers were afraid of each other, in case of informers in their ranks.

This was my first victory over the system. It gave me quite a boost and encouraged me to go further. I have described how I protested to the commandant about the impossible conditions in cell sixteen. Shortly afterwards, some of the prisoners were moved out. But it was not long before once again the numbers were again increased to five. I promptly lodged another protest with the police, and I knew that the consul had also protested on my behalf to the appropriate ministry in Prague. I decided that if they persisted in rejecting this request, I would not eat until they did something about it. That night I refused my evening meal. When breakfast came around, I refused that also, and asked that the matter should be reported on my official papers and also to the consul and the commandant. About an hour later, the officer in charge came back to report that there had been a high-level conference of the six senior prison officers to discuss my case. If I did not end my fast, it would have to be reported to the Ministry of Justice, to the Ministry of the Interior, and to the president of the court where I was to be tried in a few days' time. He pleaded with me to eat something, promising to go away personally and heat up my coffee and bring fresh bread. The fifth man would be taken away immediately. Having made my point, I consented, to the intense pleasure of my cellmates. By standing up to authority in circumstances where they could not, I had made their day, boosted morale, and stirred the feeling of human dignity.

I tried the same tactics again, without success, shortly before Christmas. I had asked permission to write extra letters to members of my family besides the official one a fortnight, which of course always went to Zena. Permission granted, I wrote to my brothers, my sister, my mother, and my daughters — only to have the duty officer refuse to take them. Deaf to my disappointed pleading, he only threatened me with the punishment cell, which meant the dungeons and half rations. He also refused to let me speak to the commandant. I immediately went on a hunger strike, but after three days I realized it was by then too late to get the letters away for Christmas. Authority had won that round.

But on the matter of overcrowding, I had won. From that time on, whenever they tried to put an extra man into our cell, I protested strongly and they always gave in. These small gestures are important in human terms.

I was now launched on a regular counteroffensive to obtain my rights and every possible privilege as well. Because I was a Christian, it did not mean I had to lie down meekly and take all that they did to me. Letters from Christians all over the world gave me encouragement. I was not alone, not forgotten. Even the prison officers were aware that the eyes of the world were watching. They complained of all the letters I was receiving, but they could not stop them. At that stage, before I was sentenced, there were no restrictions on a prisoner's incoming mail.

During the interrogation sessions, as I became increasingly aware of their methods, I was able, by being deliberately evasive in my replies, to draw out of them information which told me how much they actually knew of the work of missions taking literature behind the Iron Curtain. Also, by now I had realized that all their accusations were designed to put me on the defensive, so that they could establish in advance of my trial any defense that I might be able to produce. This would enable them to prepare witnesses to counter my arguments. So I led them astray, telling them much that was irrelevant, while in the meantime preparing a defense which I could spring on them in the courtroom. This proved successful, in that I was acquitted of all charges except that of sedition.

I was very angry at the outcome of my trial. How could they find me guilty of a political charge because of the Bibles? A Czech prisoner volunteered the address of the Ministry of Foreign Affairs in Prague. That decided me; I would write a strong letter of protest to the minister. To make sure it was delivered, I took the precaution of sending a copy to Mr. McCallion, and paid for both letters to be registered. How much effect my protest had I do not know, but when I discussed further protests with the consul later, at the appeal court, he told me he thought my original letter was sufficiently strong and comprehensive.

At least, I thought to myself, it showed I was not taking this treatment lying down.

After I had been transferred to Prague I continued the protest further. I realized that the strain of uncertainty was causing Zena to suffer as much as I was. In addition, I had just received a letter from my brother Aubrey, who was looking after the business, indicating that there were many pressing problems which could not be dealt with until my return. I nearly burst with sheer frustration. I wrote a long letter of protest to the consul, addressed personally to Mr. McCallion, stressing my desperation, and pointing out the obvious fact that the longer I stayed in prison the greater would be the resultant publicity in the West. I expressed surprise that the authorities could not see this: "Isn't there anyone in this country capable of understanding what effect this will have on Czechoslovakia?" I added that the publicity caused by the closing of the travel company would in itself be sure to stir up a great deal of anti-Communist propaganda.

Two days later the censor sent me a message that this letter could not be sent to the consul, because he "would not be able to help me." However, whereas other letters rejected by the censor were returned to the writer, this letter was never given back to me. Other prisoners who knew about it agreed with me that it must have been sent to the Communist party officials. This, of course, was exactly what I had intended. I could not write to them directly, or they would have made a fresh accusation against me, but if they were rude enough to read my personal letters to the consul, well. . . . I had one secret weapon with which the authorities could not interfere — prayer. They could censor my letters, they could even refuse me my Bible, but they could not stop me from praying. All the same, my faith was sorely tried for many months as it seemed that so many of my prayers remained unanswered. Zena was repeatedly refused permission to visit me, except for the trial. Food parcels, badly needed to supplement the prison diet, failed to arrive. The court found me guilty and sentenced me to two years.

There came a morning when I felt I could no longer pray. I sat on the hard wooden stool with its metal studs and told God, "I have prayed every prayer I can, I have no more words to use. Everything I have asked for has been refused. I don't know what else to say."

In my despair I remembered the words of the disciples: "Lord, teach us to pray." Then I thought of how Jesus had replied, "Say, Our Father . . . " (Luke 11:1,2).

Our Father. God was not distant from me. He was my Father. The reality of the relationship flooded my heart with warmth.

Which art in Heaven. No, God was not far off. He was right here in the prison cell. God was in Christ when He came down to earth, was arrested, beaten, tortured, and killed. This is the reality, God through Christ sharing our pain and suffering with us.

Hallowed be Thy name. I began to worship Him. Even though I was locked up in a cell, something of the glory of heaven came down. It seemed in that moment as if I was surrounded by all the heavenly choirs. I was no longer in the stinking room, but in the glory of the presence of Christ, singing with all the angels. No prison walls or iron bars could hold me. At that moment I was in the very presence of God Himself.

Give us this day our daily bread. How strongly this came home to me! I had been fasting in prayer. I knew what hunger was. I knew what it was like to lie awake at night unable to sleep for want of food. Dear Lord, just give me enough food for each day, to keep me alive. The words became very real to me.

Just then the cell door opened and we were ordered out

141

for the brief exercise period. I was so full of the glory and blessing of God that I just walked around and around the small exercise yard singing that wonderful hymn: "Then sings my soul, my Saviour God to Thee: How great Thou art! How great Thou art!" I was exalted. Truly God was with me. He was my Father, and in Christ He was sharing with me all this suffering. I was no longer alone or forsaken. The prison experience was worth it if only for the deeper relationship that I found with God. I seem to remember that I am not the only one to have met with God in prison.

God did not immediately answer my requests. He would continue to test my faith until in one day He gave me the accumulated answers to all my praying at once. But I never again doubted that He was with me.

14

THE GANDER AND
THE RESCUE SQUAD

For the first six months, in Bory, all my letters were censored by the SVD in charge of my interrogation. This was a constant nightmare to me, as any small slipup was added to the accusation against me.

Once I had been transferred to Prague, conditions changed. Apparently very few of the officers understood English, so they had to call on the services of the only one available whose knowledge of the language was sufficient to deal with the vast quantity of mail that was sent to me. Although I was now allowed to receive letters only from members of my family, whose names had to be individually listed with the prison authorities, many hundreds of others were sent, and they all had to be read by the censor.

During this period the censor called me for an interview and ordered me to write to my wife, telling her to put an end to all the publicity about me. They did not like all the letters which poured in protesting against my sentence. I was delighted, and in any case it was impossible to stop the flood of mail. It became a tremendous embarrassment to the Czech government and I believe this was one of the things which God was later to use to help in my expulsion.

"Why do these people keep saying that they are praying for your release?" asked the officer sarcastically. "God is dead. He cannot get you out of here. We are stronger than any God." How soon God was to prove them wrong I did not know then, any more than he did. His voice became puzzled as he went on, "We get strange letters from people who complain that you are being starved and ill-treated. What do they think our prisons are really like?" I only wished I could tell him what I thought about the prisons, but I did not dare. At least I had the satisfaction of seeing the authorities' embarrassment as it became evident that more and more people knew too much about conditions inside. By now food parcels were being sent to me from many sources, and again I was made to write to Zena and instruct her to stop them, as the publicity was bad for the image of Czech prisons. Unfortunately I was not allowed to have the parcels.

I discovered just how limited the censor's knowledge of English really was when my brother Ken came to visit me for the second time, in January. The censor had to be present in order to prevent any secret messages from being passed. He was a man of some rank, a captain or a major so far as I could guess from the unfamiliar badges, and he looked as if he was near the age for retirement. When at the end of the visit Ken gave me a food parcel from Zena and I had to list the contents for the censor, he asked me if I would tell him in German as he did not know all the English words.

On a later visit from the consul, the same man was again present, to make detailed notes of all that passed between us. As always, I had carefully jotted down all the points I wanted to raise so that nothing should be forgotten — this was important, as visits from the consul were only allowed once every two months. At the end of the interview the censor, who was obviously again in difficulties with the language, actually asked if he could borrow my notes so that he could write up the interview! I admit that I had deliberately made things awkward for him by speaking as rapidly as possible. But even so, it was clear that his knowledge of English was very small.

Naturally, I did not give him all my notes, for there were things which I had no intention of letting him see.

"We did not have time to discuss all of this, did we?" I said to Mr. McCallion.

The consul agreed.

"Then," I said, "I do not have to give him all these notes."

"No," replied the consul, "It would not be wise. Just give him half of them."

This is exactly the conversation which took place in front of the unsuspecting censor. I tore the notes in half, gave him what I thought fit for him to see, kept the rest with me, and later flushed them down the toilet.

Following this incident, I realized that I could get away with a lot with this officer. By now I was allowed to write to Zena as often as I wished, provided the letter was limited to one large page. When I could get enough stamps, I wrote daily. The other prisoners were always willing to give me stamps in exchange for some English razor blades I had found in my baggage.

Thus equipped, I began to test the censor as far as possible, writing factually about prison conditions. As I intended, this provoked him, and sometimes he would send my letter back to be rewritten, indicating the passages which he could not allow. Once I wrote: "It seems so foolish to shut men up in prisons and keep them separated from those whom they love. Men were made to be free, not imprisoned in cages like wild animals. What is it in man that makes him want to cause other men to suffer? There must be something wrong with a society that can only hold authority by fear and punishment."

This time the letter came back quickly, with this paragraph underlined in red ink. In the margin, written in red, was his comment: "I understand — but your wife, or the BBC?"

I did not destroy this part of the letter, and although I could not send it to Zena, to my surprise I was able to bring it out of the prison on the day of my release. The officers who searched me overlooked it, and it is in front of me now as I write — a remarkable testimony to the thoughts of a Communist prison officer.

On his visit, Ken had brought me a number of books, which I was not allowed to have until the censor had personally checked them for anti-Communist propaganda. Among them was James Thurber's *Fables* intended by Ken to cheer me up, and so it did. It contained several passages which were strongly satirical of the Communist system, almost on a par with *Animal Farm*, which is officially banned in all Communist states.

I was reading it one evening when a passage caught my attention. Amazed, I read it to some of the other prisoners who understood English. It was the fable of *The Rabbits Who Caused All The Trouble*.

Within the memory of the youngest child there was a family of rabbits who lived near a pack of wolves. The wolves announced that they did not like the way the rabbits were living. (The wolves were crazy about the way they themselves were living, because it was the only way to live.) One night several wolves were killed in an earthquake and this was blamed on the rabbits, for it is well known that rabbits pound on the ground with their hind legs and cause earthquakes. On another night one of the wolves was killed by a bolt of lightning and this was also blamed on the rabbits, for it is well known that lettuce-eaters cause lightning. The wolves threatened to civilise the rabbits if they didn't behave, and the rabbits decided to run away to a desert island. But the other animals, who lived at a great distance, shamed them, saying, "You must stay where you are and be brave. This is no world for escapists. If the wolves attack you, we will come to your aid, in all probability." So the rabbits continued to live near the wolves and one day there was a terrible flood which drowned a great many wolves. This was blamed on the rabbits, for it is well known that carrot-nibblers with long ears cause floods. The wolves descended on the rabbits, for their own good, and imprisoned them in a dark cave, for their own protection.

By this time other English-speaking prisoners were listening. "Do you mean to say that stuff got past the censor?" someone asked in amazement. "He must be dimmer than we thought." I went on reading:

When nothing was heard about the rabbits for some weeks, the other animals demanded to know what had happened to them. The wolves replied that the rabbits had been eaten and since they had been eaten the affair was a purely internal matter. But the other animals warned that they might possibly unite against the wolves unless some reason was given for the destruction of the rabbits. So the wolves gave them one. "They were trying to escape," said the wolves, "and, as you know, this is no world for escapists."

To men who were innocent of any real crime but were victims of a political tyranny, locked in a Communist prison, this was a safety valve. Our laughter at the satire drew the other prisoners in, so that Wolfgang had to translate for them.

By now our curiosity was aroused and we read several other pieces including *The Very Proper Gander.*

Not so very long ago there was a very fine gander. He was strong and smooth and beautiful and he spent most of his time singing to his wife and children. One day somebody who saw him strutting up and down in his yard and singing remarked, "There is a very proper gander." An old hen overheard this and told her husband about it that night in the roost. "They said something about propaganda," she said. "I have always suspected that," said the rooster, and he went around the barnyard next day telling everybody that the very fine gander was a dangerous bird, more than likely a hawk in gander's clothing. A small brown hen remembered a time when at a great distance she had seen the gander talking with some hawks in the forest. "They were up to no good," she said. A duck remembered that the gander had once told him he did not believe in anything. "He said to hell with the flag, too," said the duck. A guinea hen recalled that she had once seen somebody who looked very much like the gander throw something that looked a great deal like a bomb. Finally everybody snatched up sticks and stones and descended on the gander's house. He was strutting in his front yard, singing to his children and his wife. "There he is!" everybody cried. "Hawk-lover! Unbeliever! Flag-hater! Bomb-thrower." So they set upon him and drove him out of the country.

The book became standard reading among those in the foreign section who could read English, and was passed around from hand to hand. Either the censor had a strong sense of humor, or he had just not read the book. Here we were, condemned to brainwashing and a so-called reeducation program, and in the middle of it all we could read stories like this. Thurber's abrasive humor was a wonderful relief for us, and did much to help us keep our sanity.

Whenever someone new came into the department, out came the *Fables*. We formed a mutual rescue association, our aim a program to reeducate the reeducated.

The fact that I retained this ability to fight back against all that represented the anti-Christian Communist system helped me to maintain my mental balance. The Bible puts it like this: "We are troubled on every side, yet not distressed; we are perplexed, but not in despair; Persecuted, but not forsaken; cast down, but not destroyed" (2 Corinthians 4:8,9).

"If God be for us, who can be against us?" (Romans 8:31)

15

THE MIRAGE

Following the verdict of the appeal court, the president of the senate had announced that negotiations could now commence for my release. This at first inspired me with some hope. However, later, when I had an opportunity to discuss with the other foreigners, I found that the same thing had been said in each of their cases, with no apparent result.

I heard from my family that they were trying to arrange to visit me over the Christmas period. As both my brothers were teachers, they could only come during the school holidays. I later discovered that the British embassy had some difficulty in locating me, since nobody in the Czech Ministry of the Interior knew where I was. All that could be ascertained was that I had left Bory prison. This was very strange, as it had been an official order to transfer me to Prague. As a result of this delay, it was not until January 4 that my brothers could come to see me. Then at the last minute I heard that this date was further postponed to the eighth to allow Zena to come. This news cheered me up enormously.

A visit from one's family always entailed a lot of careful preparation. Not only did we take special care to tidy ourselves up and have a proper shave, we had to make notes of everything we wanted to say or ask, in case anything important should be forgotten. While we were on remand, we were allowed to wear our own clothes to see visitors. Now I found that we had to wear our working overalls, except when being visited by members of the embassy staff; for them we had to wear normal clothes so that the officials should not see us as we really were.

Full of elation, I was taken to the special room near the main gate where visitors were allowed. This entailed going outside the prison building, an event in itself. Ken was waiting to see me. I asked where Zena was. Ken then told me she had applied for a visa, and had travelled down to London only to be told that the Czech embassy had refused her permission for the visit. This was cruel news. Once again something I had prayed about so much was refused. It seemed as if God was always saying no to my prayers.

I had learned from the other prisoners that there was a good lawyer in Prague who specialized in getting prisoners released early, so I asked Ken to pass on an urgent message to the consul to arrange for me to have a visit from this Dr. Radl. Someone must have responded to this call, for just two days later Dr. Radl came to see me, as well as several of the other prisoners. I signed the necessary forms for an application to be made for my release. As we discussed the matter, I found out several points of interest.

When I had been sentenced, the judge had made it quite clear to me that my sentence was unconditional, so that I would have to serve the full two years. The Czechs do not observe the British system of remission, with up to a third of the sentence remitted for good conduct. On the contrary, here, far from being rewarded for good conduct, one was likely to be sent to the dungeons for minor irregularities or failure to complete the work norm.

A paragraph did exist which allowed Czech nationals to be released on parole after half the sentence, though few

151

ever got out early; there were so many things which could prevent parole. In any case, it did not apply to political prisoners, only to mere criminals. I had already met one Czech political prisoner who had completed his sentence of two years without parole, only to be rearrested as he left the prison. Apparently he had not been sufficiently reeducated during his term inside, and he was given another seven months on a trumped-up charge of making political statements about the regime.

Up till now, no foreigner had been granted parole, since we were in any case expelled at the end of our sentence, and there was no means of ensuring that parole was kept. Dr. Radl had succeeded only eight months before in fighting this issue in the local court. As a result he was arranging that as soon as Western foreigners had served half their time, an application would be made under this paragraph for their immediate release. Indeed, while I was there two Germans were released shortly after half their sentences had expired.

In my case, the earliest I could hope for release would be after twelve months. That meant June or July at the earliest. But there was one other chance, Dr. Radl explained. There remained paragraph 327 of the penal code, which allowed the authorities in exceptional circumstances to reverse the normal procedure. Instead of taking the expulsion order at the end of the sentence, it could be taken first. The procedure was complicated, involving application to two courts in Prague, getting the approval of the Foreign Ministry and the Ministry of the Interior, and the signature of the president of the republic. Finally, there had to be an allowance of at least eight days in which the prosecutor could appeal against the expulsion. All this would take two to three months at least. Dr. Radl pointed out that an application would only succeed if it had the backing of my own government through the Foreign

Office in London and the British embassy in Prague. Again, it would need constant political pressure from London. Everything would depend on the state of diplomatic relations between the two countries, and pressure brought to bear by the press and public opinion on the Foreign Office, as well as the individual efforts of MPs in the House of Commons. All I could do was to sit and wait and pray.

By the latter part of January, a glimmer of hope had appeared. The word *amnesty* began to be heard.

All over the world, wherever men are in prison, they always talk about their hopes of release. Every prisoner lives in a dream world of hope. Months ago, the boys in Bory had talked of the possibility of an amnesty. The longer their sentence, the more wildly they talked.

But this was different. Several possibilities were discussed. Someone pointed out that if a president died, the new one could declare an amnesty. Whispered comments went around on the state of President Svoboda's health. Someone else recalled a hundred-year-old tradition that if there was a new president at an election, an amnesty was always granted. Now there was new talk. February 23 would be the twenty-fifth anniversary of the founding of the Czechoslovak Socialist Republic. Perhaps an amnesty then?

As the days passed, the talk became louder, more insistent. New prisoners brought the rumors with them. Even some lawyers had mentioned the February date, sometimes in veiled hints — "Wait a few weeks and you may get good news" — at other times more positively. We even began to discuss it with the prison officers, whose noncommittal replies only added fuel to the fire; there was no outright denial. Even the most skeptical of us now began to believe there was something in the wind.

The biggest clue came from a German in my cell who

had only three months more to serve. Dieter wrote to ask his lawyer to appeal for his release, seeing that he was well past half his time. He received a reply to the effect that an appeal was unnecessary, as he would be out before an application could get to court. At this we literally jumped for joy. It was true, then! The news quickly went around the whole of our department, and all of us were to be found talking in little groups late at night when we should have been asleep. We were convinced now.

When I reflect on this, I realize that I actually prayed very little about the amnesty. I had prayed for release for nearly eight months now; this was surely the answer to all my prayers and I accepted it as such rather than continuing to pray about it. Was this the wisdom of God?

The talk was now not so much of when the amnesty would happen but of who would benefit. It was generally accepted that all of us Western foreigners would be affected. Usually, so those in the know told us, it was a question of how many years' remission would be given. Most accepted that two years would be a likely minimum, whereas four years would be about average. All of us with two years or less were fully confident. Alex, with six years, who had come in just a month before me, could at least expect to have his sentence cut. Christian, also with six years, had already served two; if it was four years, he would get out.

The final pointer came a few days before February 23. We had heard through the grapevine from some Czech prisoners that if the guards took away the television set from our work and recreation room, this would be a sign that the amnesty was on. We had the television set so that we would imbibe the constant propaganda put out, but most of us understood nothing as it was of course all in Czech. On the morning of the twenty-second, one of the prisoners standing by a window suddenly gave a shout and pointed. Sure enough, some guards were taking a television out of one of the other cell blocks.

Now we were really excited! We could hardly go on working as we watched officers come into our section and remove our set. Shortly afterwards they returned and ordered us to collect all the lead weights we had been making. Obviously they were taking these away so that we did not smash up everything in our delirious joy. I am sure some of us might have done so.

By now we discovered that we were the only ones still working. Everyone else had been given a holiday. We celebrated in the only way we knew. No work, brew up some tea, discuss plans for going home. When would we be given the news? How long would it take? Some older hands estimated that it would take about a week to release so many prisoners. The paper work would be immense. The climax came when one of the officers inadvertently admitted that the whole prison staff would be on standby over the coming weekend. This surely was it! Amnesty!

That evening shortly after supper, the officer we called Snoopy ordered a roll call. The first hint that something was wrong was in his face. No smiles. In fact he looked really miserable.

He began speaking in Czech while one of the men translated into German. It was difficult for me to follow every word but I soon got the gist of it. The amnesty had come . . . and gone. Snoopy was apologetic; he tried to be kind. He was sorry himself, he said, but what could he do? Slowly the truth sank in. We were not included in the amnesty, not one of us. Yes, one. He was a Jordanian living in West Germany who had been involved in a traffic accident while passing through Prague. He was to be released, but for the rest of us . . . no hope. We felt cheated. An immense gloom settled over the whole section. In the next few hours hardly anyone spoke, or slept. We had been condemned.

Eventually we were allowed to see the newspapers which reported the terms of the amnesty. In every case where we might have gained our freedom, Western foreigners were expressly excluded. The whole thing had been just a mirage. The officers, who I believe felt it almost as keenly as we did, told us that out of the 2,500 in our prison only forty-seven were released, and those were for minor and nonpolitical offenses. The entire prison was shocked.

About a week later, the final blow fell. Snoopy confirmed that under new laws actually enacted in the past January, no foreigners would be allowed to leave on parole at half their time. The loophole in the law had been spotted and the leak finally stopped. This, coming only a matter of days after the amnesty fiasco, was the final straw. The whole department sank to a level of despair I have never known in my life. Prisoners became sullen, listless, one or two violently aggressive. Better never to have hoped, than to have our hopes dashed in this way. Our sentences were being virtually doubled. It was at this time that I taught Wolfgang and Christian a new English phrase. We were "coming apart at the seams."

Not long after this, Snoopy came in to tell us about the new points system. This was all part of a tightening up of discipline. Now, instead of the normal routine of weekly cell inspection after intensive scrubbing, we were all lined up on inspection parade while the cells were not only inspected but searched. At the same time a system of points was instituted. For any infringement of the regulations we were given minus points, but without the possibility of offsetting these by a plus point. Minus points were given for dirty boots, not shaving, hair too long, cell windows not cleaned, dirt on the floor, dust on a ledge, a smear on a food container, and many other things. A cell receiving minus points would be punished either by loss of privileges or worse, a period in the dungeons. We were able to extract a little amusement from all this. For dirty boots we got three points, for failing to wash ourselves, only one. This seemed typical of the Communists, they always get their priorities wrong. Their ideology keeps the workers' boots clean, but overlooks their unwashed faces.

In the weeks that followed, one thing dominated our thoughts. Our lawyers would not come to see us. The new measures and the amnesty mirage had destroyed all hopes of our early release. Not even Dr. Radl could help us. The only ones who went out were those whose sentences ended. For the rest of us, life became harder and more difficult to bear. Our last hope was now gone. The whole department had "come apart at the seams."

16

PAUL AND SILAS DIDN'T
DO IT THIS WAY

After the fiasco of the amnesty I felt lower than ever. I had tried to keep a regular prayer time, but this was difficult as it was almost impossible ever to be alone. I could not kneel by my bed; there was no room, and in any case the guards, watching through the spy holes, would soon have stopped me. I tried praying in bed. This was not satisfactory. I found it easier to concentrate my thoughts while walking up and down the corridor outside the cell, thus exercising both soul and body. Unfortunately, someone would nearly always fall in and walk alongside me to chat about something. To find peace in my soul, I craved direct contact with God, a whole night of prayer.

I tried staying awake until the others were asleep. But every time I tried, someone was moving about or talking until the early hours. There was only one way, to wake up in the middle of the night, and then get up to pray. But how could I be sure of waking? Only one answer to that. I would miss my last visit to the toilet, and the physical discomfort would wake me. With this crude alarm system I started my nights of solitary prayer.

I have always believed in the scriptural injunction to fast as well as pray. There are times when one is too concerned to eat, so you pray instead; there are also times when words are inadequate and you are desperately burdened before God for something, and it is then that I fast. It helps to show God that I really mean business. I don't mean simply missing a meal, or making do with bread and cheese. To me, fasting means no food at all for a minimum of twenty-four hours, sometimes much longer. In my desperate state, I had to take desperate action. The food we had was terrible and I was often hungry and weak from want, but I determined to do this extra. I fasted for four days, then had a break, then for another two days. In addition I fasted each Sunday. Out of thirty days I fasted ten, while for the other twenty I existed on what I could salvage from the prison fare plus what came in parcels.

During this time I had a real consciousness that God was with me. Yet still the despair continued until one night, in a moment of extremity, I told God that I would do anything, absolutely anything, if only He would get me out of here. My mind was still reeling under the impact of the amnesty, the failure of my family to secure my release, my lawyer's refusal to see me, the apparent failure of the British Foreign Office to intervene.

Up till now, the other prisoners had encouraged me by saying that the British government was sure to act. They pointed out that two Swedish prisoners had been released on the intervention of their government. Pro-British feeling had been apparent at first, but now even that was waning. Now I was being taunted with failure. No one cared, Britain was no longer great. Even Czechoslovakia could twist the lion's tail. But God could help me. Prayer is more powerful than politics. The Communists could twist the tail of a weakened Britain, but not that of an omnipotent God. This was the challenge I put to him. Everyone else had failed; now let God reveal Himself by intervening on my behalf. I repeated my promise that I would do anything He asked, if only He would get me out. That was a dangerous thing to do; now things would happen.

A few days later, Jan Wildhagen, from Holland, suggested that I should hold a service for the prisoners. We talked with some of the others and eventually got together eight who would like to take part. But first I must ask the brigadier, Rudi, since it must be done openly. He was in favor, provided he got permission from the officers; it was too risky otherwise. Surprisingly, one of the kinder officers agreed to allow it.

How were we to conduct the service? Language was no problem; I would speak in English and someone would translate into German. We could pray, but what about a Bible to read from? Way back in Bory, I had received a letter from someone in Stoke-on-Trent, with no address and containing only words from the New English Bible. I had looked at the signature, Paul, and wondered who had written it as I did not know anyone of that name in Stoke. A few days later another letter arrived, this time signed Paul and Ruth. The following letters gave the clue, for when one was signed David, I realized that the signature was an indication of the biblical book from which the quotations were taken. In all, I received seven, all containing nothing but Scripture, all written on a Gospel writing pad from Hong Kong with Chinese characters quoting a text. This must have mystified the censor, who probably thought the letters came from China. I had no idea who was sending these letters, only that they were a blessing to me. Six months after my release, I was speaking in the town hall in Hanley, Stoke-on-Trent, telling this story and to my great joy Freda and Reg Allman came to me afterwards to tell me they had written the letters. They were still able to give me the exact references of the verses which they had sent. When I had no Bible, these letters contained enough Scripture to enable me to conduct a service. How wonderfully God provides!

The service was held on a Saturday. We had requested a Sunday, but this had been refused. We held it in the room where we did our work during the week. At the same time, the other prisoners were allowed out to play volleyball, a very special treat as normally we were not allowed out at all on Saturdays or Sundays. At first eight men 'had indicated their desire to attend, but when they heard the other condition the number dropped to only four. Those who attended had to give their names to the prison officers. This and the promise of a game of volleyball soon changed their minds.

However, four of us met quietly. Besides myself, there was another Englishman, Roger, who was in for drug smuggling, Jan from Holland, in for trying to smuggle out his East German fiancée, and Rudi from Germany. Together we prayed and read the Bible letters. It was wonderful to feel that there, surrounded by atheistic Communists, we could worship God. Afterwards several of the others begged to borrow the Bible letters and so the Word of God was passed around from one to another all unknown to the prison officers. The letters were eagerly read. These men were not all Christians, but as one said to me, "It is only when you are in a place like this that you realize how much you need God." That brief service and the letters revealed Christ to several who never knew Him before. Even Alex, who had been quite a character in his past, came asking for the letters which someone translated for him. Then he told me that when he was younger he, too, had been a regular churchgoer, but had later lapsed.

This was only the beginning. Seeing the interest aroused, I went further and suggested that we should hold a regular prayer meeting. That night after roll call, eight or nine men crowded into my cell, one third of the whole department. Some were drug smugglers, others had criminal records, some, like me, were "political offenders." It was wonderful to hear them praying and calling on the name of the Lord night after night. My Bible tells me that "Whosoever shall call upon the name of the Lord, shall be saved" (see Acts 2:21). This went on for a number of nights, always immediately after roll call was ended and the guards had gone away. Then an informer reported us, and I was called before the officer in charge.

"What do you think you are doing?" he shouted at me. "You cannot pray here in prison, it constitutes a serious offense against the state. Why do you think we locked you up? You have been put here to stop such activities. This praying and talking about God must cease immediately. If not, you will be charged with subversion and you will get another five years."

This was almost unbelievable! Five years extra for praying — and they claim there is religious freedom in Czechoslovakia! I did not intend to stop the prayer meetings and there were others who agreed with me, though some withdrew. We agreed to continue, but changed the time to early morning before work. Those meetings did not stop until the day I left. Jan, Rudi, and I, often just the three of us, sometimes more, kept up the regular chain of prayer. God is stronger than the Communists. They could not stop us, for does not the hymn writer say, "Satan trembles when he sees the weakest saint upon his knees"?

Now I was beginning to really call upon God for help. So far, it seemed, everything I asked for had been refused. Not that God would not answer, but I had to learn that sometimes His answer is a definite no. Most Christians speak of answers to prayer only in the sense of getting what they want. Yet the Apostle Paul said, "I asked the Lord three times. . . . He said, My grace is sufficient" (see 2 Corinthians 12:8,9). In other words, no. For nine months I had been on the receiving end of God's refusals. But this did not stop me from asking, it only increased my determination.

On March 27 I had another visit from the consul, during which I mentioned that I had frequently been refused permission to get some things from my suitcases. Snoopy, who was among the prison officers monitoring our interview, was the chief offender, and I was really trying to embarrass him into action, for there were no real grounds for his refusal.

Immediately the interview was ended, but instead of going back to my cell, Snoopy took me to the storeroom, where my baggage was brought out to me. I badly needed some socks, as the prison only supplied a piece of linen cloth for us to wrap around our feet. We also had to supply our own razors, with blades, and other toilet articles. The only soap provided was a coarse product which we only used for washing clothes; it was a grim prison joke that it had been left behind by the Germans after the war, with all that implied.

Right on top of one of my cases was my Bible. I picked it up lovingly. Snoopy said harshly, "Surely you have read that enough already?" I quickly said no to that. "You cannot take it to your cell," he warned. Then — deliberately or by accident? — he turned away. I thought rapidly. For nine months I had been denied this book which could bring me more comfort and help than any other. If only. . . . Why not? After all, they had put me in prison for carrying Bibles.

Quickly, with an instinctive sleight of hand, I slipped it under the arm of my overall jacket and shut the case. Snoopy turned back. Whether he saw my action or not I will never know. I walked back to the cell clutching a small selection of necessary toilet items as well as the food parcel from the consul.

I was so thrilled that I did not want to eat, sleep, or work. I had my Bible at last. I read and read as if I had never seen it before. I can understand what the believers in Communist countries feel like when they are deprived of their Bibles. This Book, which for most of my life I had taken for granted, had become the most precious thing in the world to me. I spent hours when I should have been working or cleaning, just lying on my bed, reading a book which had become alive. I was soon to experience it as literally God's Word, His voice, unchanging, undying, speaking directly to me.

Something seemed to be happening to me now. My whole relationship with God had changed, so that in my nightly prayer time I found myself communicating with Him in a way rarely possible in our normal earthbound experience. The apparent failure to secure my release, the growing tension in the prison, increasing physical weakness from poor diet and lack of exercise, the continuing mental stress which showed in physical symptoms like my heart trouble in January, all combined to make me throw myself on him without reserve.

One night, after a day more than ever frustrating, I challenged Him to answer me. "Oh, God, my Father, tell me the truth. Must I stay on here in this prison? If I must stay to the end, then tell me, but give me the grace to bear it. I will thankfully accept it. Or, if you can get me out, then tell me so, so that I can take comfort."

I called to mind a dream I had had five months before, in Bory, just two or three nights after my trial. Lying awake for long periods, sleeping only fitfully, I dreamed I was in the Royal Albert Hall in London. It was Easter Monday, for each year the Elim churches, of which fellowship I am a minister, hold a great rally on that day. In my dream, I was telling a packed congregation how wonderfully God had undertaken for me. It was as if I knew exactly what to say; something wonderful had happened. When I woke up I dismissed the dream as fantasy, and it was soon forgotten in the face of the problem of survival.

Now suddenly I remembered the dream. I began to pray more specifically. "It seems impossible, God, but you specialize in the impossible. . . . Tell me if I can go home for Easter."

The next day I went on with my surreptitious Bible reading. I was reading through the Psalms. David, the psalmist, had experienced a very rough time, I thought, so perhaps here I would find some comfort. I had gotten as far as Psalm 35, when the words of verse 18 seemed to leap out at me: "I will give thee thanks in the great congregation: I will praise thee among much people." Surely here was my answer. The Royal Albert Hall seats eight thousand. Truly a "great congregation"!

This was wonderful news, and I thought about it for a day or two. I was working something out in my mind. "If I am to be actually in the Albert Hall on a Monday, I can hardly be going home on that day, it must be a day earlier. But they don't release prisoners on Saturdays or Sundays. It must be that I'll leave on Good Friday."

That night as I paced the corridor I suddenly became very cheeky. I said to God, "You have promised to have me home for Easter Monday, that is April 23. Why can't I go home for my birthday, on the seventeenth?" Well, nothing could stop me from asking. God could say no, or yes, but at least I could ask Him.

I fell asleep repeating the question over and over again: "Please, God, may I go home for my birthday?" In the morning as soon as I woke I began to pray again: "If I am to go home for my birthday, show me by another verse from the Bible. Show me one where it says You release a prisoner bound with chains." I took up my Bible and continued reading. I came to Psalm 68:6: "God setteth the solitary in families: he bringeth out those which are bound with chains." This was exactly what I had asked for. I was absolutely convinced. "I'm going home for my birthday!" I was so excited I could hardly contain my joy. I was certain it was true. Well, who wouldn't get excited at a promise as wonderful as that?

Yet there was more to follow. Remember, up until now God had nearly always said no to my requests. I am sure this was to test my trust in Him to the extreme limit. Now He was piling promise upon promise. I read on through the Psalms. This time it was Psalm 119 that helped me. One phrase appears repeatedly — "according to thy word." You find it at least seven times in different contexts, particularly in verse 170: "Let my supplication come before thee: deliver me according to thy word." This was confirmation of the previous promises. I need have no more doubts, for the promise of my release was according to His Word. I read and reread these verses and my soul became filled with peace and certainty. The Bible is God's Word and cannot lie; then it must happen even as He promised. All the promises of man are meaningless compared to the might and power of God. He is greater than the Communists. Did He not release Paul and Silas from prison in Philippi? Did He not also release Peter? Well, was God any different now? Was His power diminished? God never changes, nor do His promises. I, for one, would believe.

It was March 31 when this promise was given to me. The next days I spent in a real joy of anticipation, knowing that God would not fail. Yet, locked in that prison, seeing every day the iron bars, hearing the shouted commands, and feeling the oppressive mood of the prisoners, it was not easy to keep believing. There still remained one last challenge. I must witness to some of the other prisoners and tell them I was going home, so that when the moment came they could know that it was God's promise which was being fulfilled. I had to be careful whom I told and

166

how I told them. No use making it into a joke, so quietly I told those I could trust, not all the details nor the exact date, just the fact that I would be going home soon.

It was during this period that we came to Friday, April 13. The day started as all the others had before it, with work as usual, but somehow during the morning things went very wrong. My nerves were at breaking point. I supposed it was the tension between my belief that I would soon be home and the fact that there was no earthly reason for such a hope. I was sitting at my bench working; there was a great deal of noise, one of the Germans was talking loudly, the others were laughing. I felt lost. I could not understand what was going on, the accent of the Berliner was strange, nothing was coherent, just a babel of sound coming at me. I got up from my stool. I could stand it no longer. Slamming the door I rushed to my cell, shaking violently.

How can I describe what happened? Everything was pressing in on me. In fact, my breakdown was not surprising; this was the inevitable outcome of months of strain and tension. Others had long ago resorted to medical attention, psychiatric treatment, and drugs. I had held out until now.

Fortunately both Christian and Wolfgang, who worked on either side of me, realized immediately what had happened. They were kind and helpful. Wolfgang gave me some sleeping tablets and tranquilizers offered by another prisoner. The shaking and trembling persisted until I dropped off to sleep.

When I woke later that afternoon the full realization of what had happened hit me hard. Here I was, believing that I would soon be free, yet I had broken down like this. I ought to be rejoicing. If I really believed God's promise, would I have collapsed?

I lay on my bed with the tears running down my cheeks.

167

"Oh, God, forgive me for failing You. Don't be angry with me. Don't let me spend another fourteen months in prison just for losing control. I'm only human, the tension was too much. Forgive me. Surely You understand, Father! Don't turn Your face from me now." I could not claim any strength of my own, only what He could give me. Gradually I felt the peace come flooding back into my soul, a new sense of harmony with God. I knew that He had seen my tears and heard the cry of my heart. He knows the very depths of our soul. This had been for me a Gethsemane experience: "Not my will, but thine, be done" (Luke 22:42).

The next day was Saturday, but it was an extra work day. We had these several times, usually in order to donate aid to the Vietcong, "struggling against the American imperialists." Czechoslovakia specialized in supplying small arms and ammunition to revolutionaries throughout the world, including Ireland, to aid them in the "struggle for peace." On Friday, Christian, Wolfgang, and Hermann had covered up for me, doing my share of the work so that I would not be found out. Now I felt that I should repay them for what they had done, and show that I was fully recovered, so I not only did my own work that day but also some for each of them.

I also felt challenged to prove to God that I was taking Him at His word, so I began to prepare my few personal possessions for going home. Letters and papers which I did not want to fall into the hands of the authorities I tore up and flushed down the toilet. I wrote up my diary, which I had kept since the day of my arrest. On Sunday I continued with these various jobs, sorting out my uniform and making a pile of my own things. The final and most important task was to hide my diary so that it would not be discovered when they searched me before leaving. For a long time I had experimented with hiding places, and had decided that a toothpaste or shampoo tube would be best. I had then tried the effect of shampoo versus toothpaste on the paper and ink, and decided that the shampoo did the least damage. I had been able, on the occasion when I was allowed access to my baggage, to bring a tube into my cell. Carefully I squeezed some out, washed and dried the tube, then tightly rolling the closely written notes I pushed them through the neck of the tube. Once inside, a little shake opened the roll out to fill the width of the tube. Then to complete the job, a little shampoo was poured back in, to fool any guard who might try to squeeze it.

During that weekend four of the other prisoners separately took me on one side to caution me against overoptimism. There could be no hope of my release, they said. They were afraid that constant anticipation of an impossibility would undermine my health. In view of my behavior on Friday, they were quite justified. But they could not understand, nor could I explain fully, though I tried, what God's promise meant to me.

I slept fitfully on Sunday night; one half of me was excited at the prospect of reunion with Zena and the girls, the other half was endeavoring to restrain the excitement, lest it should cause a repeat of last Friday.

Monday, April 16. Work was hard. For the last few weeks we had been making flags, taking from a pile cheaply printed paper flags of the Warsaw Pact countries, gluing them, then rolling them around a wooden stick. They then had to be put under lead weights while the glue dried, collected into bundles of fifty, fastened in a special way with rubbber bands, then handed to the supervisor who would check them for faults. This seems simple enough, and it was; but the norm was 1,150 a day, and that was not so simple. In fact it was almost impossible. It needed much practice as well as nimble fingers. However, by midday I had completed about six hundred.

A few minutes before noon, Snoopy came into the department. Some of us had requested permission to draw money from our accounts to spend on the few little luxuries we were allowed to purchase once a week — things like stamps, writing paper, lard for the dry bread, cigarettes, and tobacco. I was given money to last for a whole month. Obviously there was no news of my release.

Back at my workbench, I put my head in my hands and cried silently to God in despair. He had given me a definite promise that I would be released the next day. Now it seemed impossible. Yet He had promised! God does not make mistakes. Still, humanly speaking, my hopes were shattered.

Then it seemed as if I heard God speaking to me: "David, how do you know that you are a Christian?"

I knew the answer to that. My salvation did not depend on my own feelings, nor upon my hopes — and if it was dependent on church attendance I had no chance for it was nearly ten months since I had last been to church. The answer was faith in His Word.

"The Bible says, 'Whosoever shall call on the name of the Lord shall be saved.' "

Quick as a flash the reply came into my mind. "And do you not have My promise that I will release you?"

Fresh hope rose inside me. I would go home tomorrow. God had promised. The circumstances were immaterial. God does not lie, otherwise my faith in my salvation was also in vain. I lifted my head from my hands, and as I did so I saw the clock on the wall. It was twenty past twelve.

At that exact moment, before I had even time to collect my thoughts, Snoopy came running back, calling my name. "I have just had a telephone call from the ministry." There was a pause. "You are to be released immediately."

I was speechless as the others crowded around me. This

was a miracle. Twenty minutes before, it had been impossible. Now. . . .

Snoopy went on, "You have just one hour to collect your things."

I grinned. "I don't need an hour to do that, I packed all my things last Saturday." Well, it was true enough, I had done everything I could, even to hiding my diary in the shampoo tube. There would certainly have been no opportunity to do it now, with everyone crowding around to congratulate me and say good-bye.

It was a scene I can never forget; the other prisoners in the section, sad because they must stay, but at the same time pleased for me. Christian spoke, voicing the thoughts of all of them. "No one knows that we are here, no one in the West cares. David, when you get out, tell the people in the West what conditions are like behind this Iron Curtain and in this prison."

His words remained in my mind, and I continued to hear them for a long time after I left. "No one knows and no one cares." How true that was! That is one reason this book is being written.

17

GOD OPENS PRISON DOORS

An officer came to take me out of the cells. I was given back all my belongings, my clothes, my baggage. I was handed all the mail that had come for me, uncensored for the first time.

Then he told me that I could not be freed; there had only been a telephone call, and no foreigner could be released without the necessary papers being signed. This meant that an application had to be made under paragraph 327 of the penal code, a lawyer had to present this to two courts in Prague, obtain the president's signature, then allow eight days for the chief prosecutor to appeal against my release. Normally all this would take more than two months to complete.

"Go and wait in this side room," said the officer. "We have a car going around Prague to try to complete the formalities quickly."

The time passed agonizingly slowly. I was still not a free man. At last the officer returned and, with a quick glance at me, placed a piece of paper on the table.

"Will you please sign that you are willing to leave our country?"

They must have been crazy! Of course I signed it.

Now I was given back the rest of the money in my account, which must be spent in the officers' canteen. After I had bought some boxes of chocolates for my wife and family there was still some money left over. The officer, who shall remain nameless, asked me what I wanted to do with it and I told him I would like some small personal souvenir of Czechoslovakia to take home with me. He glanced at me, hesitated, then told me to follow him. To my amazement, he took me down to the main entrance of the prison, past the guards, and out of the big gates. As I realized that I was actually seeing those grim walls from the outside, my heart beat faster. Freedom . . . only an unarmed officer by my side. . . . The sun shone brilliantly on that April afternoon, and as we walked side by side to the nearby shopping area, for the first time I began to converse with this familiar figure as a human being. He admitted, as we chatted together in German, that he realized I was no criminal, but he had only been obeying orders. Together we looked in the shop windows and I saw an ornamental coat rack made in metal shaped like a beetle on a branch. There was not much else to choose from, so I bought it, then gave the rest of the money to the officer, for his children.

It was a strange feeling to walk back voluntarily into the prison. Legally, I suppose, I was a free man, yet not free, for I must now be deported to fulfill the order of the court. I was *persona non grata* so far as Czechoslovakia was concerned.

I was taken to the escort section of the prison, the rough cells where prisoners are put on arrival, before being sent to their final quarters, or, like me, to spend their last days while awaiting release. I was not told when my actual release would come through; this must be up to other authorities whose responsibility it was to arrange the transport out of the country. According to the law, it is possible to keep a prisoner for eight days after the end of his sentence while the necessary arrangements are being made. Fortunately for me, I had written to my wife asking her to send an air ticket to the consul, one way, Prague–London, open date, valid for one year. This had been given to the prison authorities some time before and placed with my effects.

In the escort cell I was able to keep my personal things with me. They could not speak English or German here, but they brought me the first decent meal I had enjoyed for ten months, steak with rice, followed by stewed plums. Then they made signs to me that I could lie down on the bed; this was strictly forbidden in the prison cells, but now all was different. At first I did not want to lie down. However, eventually I did, when I had finally sorted and checked my things. At this they turned off the electric light, another novelty for me. So at last I fell asleep.

At six the next morning I was awakened and given the usual prison breakfast. Still no news of when I would be freed, but I gathered together all my belongings, then sat and waited. It was twenty minutes past seven by my watch, which had been returned to me, when three plain-clothes officers of the SVD came to the cell, took me out, searched all my baggage again, then escorted me to a waiting car.

I looked out of the windows as we travelled across the city. Where are we going? I thought. Surely this is not the way to the airport? I saw a road sign for Pilsen. The airport is in the opposite direction, I am sure; where are we going? For a few moments a horrifying thought attacked me. Perhaps these men will take me back to Bory, then start a fresh charge against me; more interrogation and a new trial. I well knew that nothing was impossible in this country. These men were the SVD; they could do what they liked with me. The other prisoners had told me I would not actually be free until I stepped on to the aircraft, and then not if it was a Czechoslovak plane. That was why my ticket was made out BEA.

At last, gazing anxiously out of the car window, I saw the familiar signpost with an aircraft, which in international language meant that the car was travelling in the right direction. We drew up outside the entrance and I was escorted in, my baggage taken away by the staff. Strangely, at no time was I allowed to handle either my air ticket or my passport before boarding the aircraft. Waiting around in the lounge with my escort, I saw the vice consul from the British embassy, Mr. Woodruff, who was allowed to speak to me for a few minutes. He told me that Mr. Harold Wilson, Labor leader, past prime minister (and soon to be again), would probably be on the same plane.

At last I was allowed to climb the steps into the plane. I sat in the front section watching as the usual airport bus drove up with the other passengers. Just a few men got on board; they sat opposite me, then one came and asked if he might sit next to me, unusual in an almost empty plane. He held out his hand and said, "Mr. Hathaway, I presume." Then the storm broke. They all clamored around me. These were newspaper reporters who had been in the country to cover a story to do with education. Perhaps they had heard a rumor about me, I do not know. They introduced themselves and started a news conference on the spot. That was when the stewardess came to tell me that Mr. Wilson was in the rear compartment and would like me to sit with him. The reporters asked me if he had had anything to do with my release. I told them I did not know.

Throughout the flight, Mr. Wilson was very kind. I found him most pleasant and warmhearted. He even sent his agent, seeing I had no money, to ask if he could buy a present for my wife. We were both delighted with the bottle of perfume Mr. Wilson gave me for her, a small gesture but at that moment it meant a great deal.

Mr. Wilson told me that he had flown to Czechoslovakia to make an important speech; they had pressed him many times, but this was the first time he had been free to go. Then apparently the day before, at one o'clock, he had been a guest at an official lunch and he had made a special request for me to be released in time to fly home on the same flight next day. It was only after I returned home that I realized the significance of this timing. Mr. Wilson's request had been made at one, the prison officer had come for me at twelve twenty — forty minutes earlier!

As I stepped off the plane at London airport, I looked at my watch. It was 10:45 A.M. on April 17. It was my birthday, exactly as God had promised me. He never fails! The final confirmation came three or four hours later. I had gone straight to my sister's home in Cheltenham to see my aged mother. The telephone rang. It was the Elim churches. Would I be willing to speak in the Royal Albert Hall on Easter Monday? So God confirmed both promises from the Bible in the most wonderful way. He even sent Mr. Wilson, a prime minister of Great Britain, to fetch me out in fulfillment of His perfect plan and purpose.

Naturally Zena, my brothers, and my sister were all at the airport to greet me. I was taken into a press conference with Mr. Wilson, but as we went in the door, we were warned that two members of the Czech embassy staff were present, so this and Mr. Wilson's request to me not to embarrass him or the Foreign Office kept me quiet about true conditions in Czechoslovakia. In truth, although I was bursting to tell the whole story, I must confess that I was at that moment extremely grateful to the Czech government for releasing me, especially as it was in fulfillment of a promise from the Bible which they so despised.

18

IMPRISONED FOR HIS GLORY

It was not until after I came out of prison that I was able to piece together the full story behind my arrest and the events which led to my release.

Things had first begun to go wrong on the night we arrived in Wurzburg, Tuesday, June 20. I had understood that the other members of our courier team would be arriving with the load of Bibles at about 9:00 P.M. When eleven o'clock came and they had still not put in an appearance, David Lowth and I decided to go to bed. We had had little rest the previous night on the cross-channel ferry, and we were aware that the following night would be spent in unloading and distributing the literature. Understandably we felt disturbed at the thought of three broken nights in a row. In view of the uncertainty of our contacts ever arriving, I arranged with Will Dickerson and Peter Harvey who, travelling as passengers, were assisting us with the Bibles, to wait up and supervise the loading.

The Bibles did arrive, in the early hours of the morning while I was asleep, and were duly loaded. I had no knowledge whatever of the contents of the boxes, nor had Will or Peter. So far as I was aware, the whole consignment was of Czech Bibles, in response to a request brought out of Czechoslovakia by one of the team members.

From the moment of the discovery at the Czech border

I had maintained that I did not know the contents of the compartment, and this was quite true, though my interrogators never did believe me. Statements from some of the passengers confirmed that I had gone to bed before the boxes had arrived. However, neither Will nor Peter divulged the fact that they had been responsible for the actual loading, and I did not mention this to the secret police; it was enough that I was being held, without any others becoming involved. As the owner of the travel company I had to accept a certain amount of responsibility, otherwise the passengers might not have been released.

Who then did put the leaflet *Proč?* on the bus? It must have been the members of the support team, who alone had detailed knowledge of what they had brought.

Since my release I have heard many rumors that there was a tip-off, that either someone deliberately betrayed me or else the men were seen in the process of loading that night in Germany. If there was no information passed to the Czechs, it is argued, then how did they find the Bibles when we had operated so successfully for so long?

I have investigated every possible source of information to satisfy myself on those very questions. If there had been a slipup, if someone had betrayed me, then for the protection of all believers I wanted to know. Could it have been information from within our security-conscious organization? Did someone deliberately want to "shop" me? If either of these were the case, then I needed to find out, for the safety of the other couriers as well as of those behind the Iron Curtain.

There was definitely no information or tip-off given to the border guards. Of this I am absolutely certain after exhaustive investigation and much thought. If there had been, the border police would not have taken so long to find the Bibles. Neither would they have waited nearly seven hours before bringing in the SVD. If they thought that I was guilty, why did they at first hold the driver in custody and not even take me in for questioning until about 10:00 P.M.? We had arrived at the crossing point at three in the afternoon. Another important point is that if they knew in advance that we had Bibles, they would have let us enter, then followed us. Then they would have arrested all our contacts, the believers, and ourselves.

How then and why, was I caught? The answer is apparently very simple, and is confirmed both by the transcript of the evidence of the customs officer at my trial and by my own inquiries.

As I have explained, this Bible run was to have followed a new pattern of multiple deliveries which we had successfully developed, crossing back and forth over the borders between Western and Eastern countries and making our final pickup in Yugoslavia before crossing into Rumania. The consignment for Yugoslavia was taken across the border from Austria in other vehicles with which we had a rendezvous at a comfortable hotel in the little village of Sremska Mitrovia, off the main road between Zagreb and Belgrade. It was such a quiet location that there was no difficulty in finding a secluded place nearby to load the bus.

This time we were working with a new team of support vehicles and workers, who like the previous teams were from Underground Evangelism. In order to transport the Bibles over the Yugoslav frontier, I had been asked to bring some empty suitcases in which to pack them. These were to have been taken off the bus at Wurzburg, but I found when I opened up the bus in the morning that the team had taken only a few, leaving the rest with me.

So we were forced to set off for the Czech frontier with a load of spare suitcases. At a lunch stop before the border Will and I tried to disguise some of them by filling them with food which we had brought along for picnic supplies.

Others we packed with coats and other loose items from the bus, and we finally threw some into a neaby ditch. However we had to approach the frontier with seventeen passengers (the planned number) whose cases were neatly stowed, but having in addition a number of other cases which had to be put into the side lockers and even overflowed into the interior of the bus.

Hence my apprehension as we approached the border, and particularly when I saw the thorough search of the bus ahead. As it turned out, my fears were well founded. The customs officer admitted in evidence that his suspicions were first aroused by the obvious surplus of cases, which was unusual, as the bus and compartment were designed to carry either fifty passengers, or twenty passengers plus the Bibles, with plenty of room for baggage.

Looking back, I could think of many things which nearly prevented us from ever setting out on that tour, including a mysterious sudden brake failure which was only just repaired in time. As I pondered these things in prison, I concluded that either God had a deliberate purpose in allowing me to be imprisoned, or I was out of His will and He had been trying to prevent me from making the trip. I am now convinced that He had allowed this experience for His glory, and this certainty remained with me through even the most despairing moments of my imprisonment. It was confirmed by the way He subsequently revealed Himself to me, and even more by the miraculous way in which He brought about my release. Zena and I both remain convinced that, harrowing though the experience was, it was God's purpose to allow me to go to prison so that He might have greater glory through the story of my miraculous release being told all over the world; I also believe that it was His purpose to give me personal experience of the suffering of the believers behind the Iron Curtain, so that it might focus the attention of the

Christians in the West on the plight of the Persecuted Church.

The pressure for my release began to build up almost from the time my arrest was made known. From the beginning I was convinced, and so were my fellow prisoners, that the only way to obtain my release was to create as much publicity as possible back home in England. However, the Foreign Office in London thought otherwise. As soon as the news of my arrest reached my wife, they asked her not to mention it to anyone, especially not the press. They were so insistent over this that poor Zena waited several days before she even dared to tell my family.

Joe Bass and Underground Evangelism wanted to help in every way possible, and were active right from the beginning. However, they were hampered by the fear that if my connection with them were known to the SVD, I would be blamed for even more activities than those I was now accused of. The extent of our cooperation could not be revealed until I had returned home. In the meantime they did all they could to help Zena and the girls, and supported all Zena's efforts towards my release.

In the letter I managed to give to Zena at the time of my trial, I indicated that she should go ahead with all possible publicity. As was inevitable, when she and Ken returned after the trial, it was to a barrage of publicity in the press and on television. One outcome of this was the flood of letters and food parcels which were sent to me in prison; over 3,000 letters were actually sent, though I was not allowed to receive them all. They came from all over the world, many from young people, students, churches, and other groups. All protested about my imprisonment and assured me of the writers' prayers for my release.

At the same time, my family had written letters and made appeals on my behalf to Christians everywhere. Every member of the House of Commons was approached. Ken took charge of this side of the task while my other brother, Aubrey, who lives not far from our home, helped with the affairs of the business. Zena herself was fully occupied with all the correspondence involved. After my release I looked up in Hansard the many questions which were asked by members of Parliament concerning my case. I had known, while in prison in Prague, that there were going to be questions in the House of Commons, since the consul had visited me on January 26 specifically to obtain the latest facts for inclusion in the answers. At the time of his visit, he was able to tell me that the Czechs were becoming embarrassed by the whole affair, which cheered me very much.

After I came home, there was a good deal of press controversy over who had actually gotten me out of prison. In all fairness to the parties concerned, I must try to relate something of the events immediately prior to my release. I have done everything possible to ascertain the facts, but I realize that I cannot possibly name everyone who played a part. I am most grateful to all who were involved, however small or great their contribution. One newspaper summed it up accurately in the midst of all the controversy, by saying that the most important thing was not who did what, but that I was out.

The week before my homecoming, the deputy Czech foreign minister flew to London for talks with Sir Alec Douglas Home at the Foreign Office, and I know that my case and the possibility of my release were discussed. Also, in that same week, a representative of the British Council of Churches was invited to attend a reception at the Czech embassy, and again my case was raised with the same official. As a result of these and other pressures, my family was given some indication that I might soon be expelled. In the midst of this, Mr. Harold Wilson, then Leader of the Opposition, accepted an invitation to fly to Prague and speak at a special function.

Mr. Wilson personally made his plea for my release on Monday, April 16, requesting that if assurance had been given of my expulsion at an early date, they should take the positive step releasing me in time to fly home with him on the 9:00 A.M. flight out of Prague the next day. It is obvious to me that they did just this. The haste of my expulsion could not be explained in any other way. The Foreign Office clearly must have received some assurance, but Mr. Wilson personally brought me home. I shall always be grateful to him.

Throughout all this activity, one factor stands out more than anything else. This is the way in which Christians everywhere were praying for me. The final miracle of my release must be attributed first and foremost to the power and effective influence of prayers from Christians all over the world. It was God who released me.

What thrilled me above all was that, all the time I was in Czechoslovakia, the Communists had been telling me that it was no use praying to a dead God. Prayer could not get me out of prison, and there was no point in reading the Bible because it was only dead history. Yet God triumphed over the Communists by bringing me out of the prison in direct answer to prayer, and in doing so, in fulfillment of His plan and purpose, He used someone as important as a leading British politician. How great and wonderful He is, to use people in high places to help a Bible courier, in answer to your prayers and mine.

Many people ask me what I am doing now. At the time of my trial, I had asked God to give me definite guidance about what I was to do when I was eventually released. It had been a miracle all those years ago which had brought me into the travel business. It seemed that this career had now ended, but I could not give it up without definite confirmation from God. I asked Him for a clear sign. I prayed that, if He wanted me to continue in the travel business, He would tell me by leaving me to serve my full sentence. But if He wanted me to leave the travel business and had a mission for me to carry out in my life, then I asked that He would perform another miracle of His love and secure my release.

When He did so, I knew what I must do. I have disposed of my former business, and am now giving my full life and energies in a total commitment to help the Persecuted Church.

This is perhaps why God allowed me to suffer with them; to have only a small understanding of their hardship, suffering, and sacrifices.

I can never be the same, having seen them, shared with them, and gone through the troubled waters of suffering they pass through daily. I am involved full time in helping to share God's Word with the millions of our fellow Christians in Communist lands who are denied it. Underground Evangelism has long since replaced "Albert" with other very good means of taking Bibles and help to the Persecuted Church. Obviously, I cannot say too much, except that this most important work moves ahead with God's blessings. It's not through man's cleverness that this is possible but because God has heard every anguished prayer of His children.

He cares! We depend totally upon Him, rather than on man's ingenuity, and He never fails, for His love knows no barriers, acknowledges no Iron Curtain, and recognizes no man-made obstacles.

The question I am often asked is: Would I do it all again if I knew in advance the price I would have to pay? I have often thought of that question. I have looked at my little daughter Mandy playing, and the twins at the age when a father's help is so needed. I have so often thought of

Zena, who went through far more as a wife and mother than I could imagine, carrying such a heavy load all alone. Then I think of those seemingly endless, long nights in Communist prisons when despair and hopelessness filled the tiny cell.

And yet my answer has to be: "Yes, I would do it all again." I'm not a hero, nor do I make claims to any special bravery. I have my fears and trepidations, like anyone. But when one sees the suffering of our fellow Christians in Communist lands; the desperate hunger for Bibles which compels them to travel hundreds of miles in search of a single Scripture portion; when one sees young new believers pleading for a few pages of Scriptures to start out their Christian life; when one sees pastors having to preach God's Word from a few tattered notebook pages with Scriptures pencilled in from memory; when one sees the destitute wives and children of men imprisoned for their faith — then there can only be one answer to that question.

I remember trudging endlessly around the grim prison exercise yard, seemingly in an impossible situation . . . yet from somewhere within the depths of my soul, I sang out the words of that beloved song, "How Great Thou Art."

How Great Thou Art

Then sings my soul, my Savior God to thee;
How great thou art, how great thou art!
Then sings my soul, my Savior God to thee;
How great thou art, how great thou art!

CARL BOBERG
STUART K. HINE (Translator)

And now, I am out . . . and free; yet **they are still there** paying a daily price of suffering, but He is great enough to hear their prayers.

Those persecuted, suffering believers are my brothers and sisters. **They are yours as well.** The Bible says that at the final judgment, men shall say, "Lord, when did we see You hungry, and naked and sick, and in prison and help You?" And the Lord will answer and say, "Verily I say unto you, inasmuch as you have done it unto one of the least of these My brethren, ye have done it unto Me" (*see* Matthew 25:37-40).

Having been with them, worked with them, and been privileged to share only a little of the suffering they pass through, **I appeal to you not to forget them.** They don't ask for their suffering to be lifted, nor for their crosses to be lightened. They count it a privilege when called upon to suffer for His sake. But they do ask not to be forgotten.

The cry of the Persecuted Church still rings in my ears: "Nobody knows what is happening to us and no one cares about us. David, tell them what you have seen and heard, so that we are not forgotten by the Christians in the West."

I have told what I saw and heard. I have kept my promise to them.

Will they be forgotten?

That question is between you and God.

The author invites correspondence and gifts to provide Bibles and help for the Persecuted Church in Communist lands. The address is:

David Hathaway
Underground Evangelism
P.O. Box 808
Los Angeles, California 90053

or

David Hathaway
Underground Evangelism
Box 1296
Calgary, Alberta, Canada
T2P 2L2